Restoration

D. THOMAS LANCASTER

RETURNING THE TORAH OF MOSES TO THE DISCIPLES OF JESUS

For truly I say to you, until heaven and earth pass away, not the smallest letter or stroke shall pass from the Law until all is accomplished.
— Matthew 5:18

Restoration

D. THOMAS LANCASTER

RETURNING THE TORAH OF MOSES TO THE DISCIPLES OF JESUS

First Fruits of Zion is a 501(c)(3) registered nonprofit educational organization.

Fourth Edition 2015
Printed in the United States of America

ISBN: 978-1-941534-01-4

Cover design: Avner Wolff

Quantity discounts are available on bulk purchases of this book for educational, fundraising, or event purposes. Special versions or book excerpts to fit specific needs are available from First Fruits of Zion. For more information, contact www.ffoz.org/contact.

First Fruits of Zion

Israel / United States / Canada

PO Box 649, Marshfield, Missouri 65706–0649 USA
Phone (417) 468–2741, www.ffoz.org

Comments and questions: www.ffoz.org/contact

RESTORATION 2015.INDD; 12-02-2015; RESTORATION 2015_V6_PRESS.PDF

TO MARIA ANNE
אשת חיל
AND SOUL COMPANION

AND IN LOVING MEMORY OF
LORRAINE DELORES LANCASTER,
A TRUE DISCIPLE OF THE KING

Contents

PROLOGUE

The Tenth Anniversary Edition

First Fruits of Zion released the first edition of *Restoration: Returning the Torah of God to the Disciples of Jesus* in 2005. We wanted an easy-to-read book that could introduce readers to the ideas behind Messianic Judaism and the Jewish Roots movement in Christianity. Since then the book has sold through several printings and impacted many lives.

All my other books combined have not sold so many copies as *Restoration,* nor have they garnered so much response. At First Fruits of Zion, we continually receive testimonies from Christian readers telling us about how the book opened their eyes to the Scriptures and changed their perspectives. Many report a renewed passion for God, for the Bible, and the life of godliness. Enthusiastic readers often order multiple copies, sometimes whole cases of the book, to distribute to their family and friends. In these respects, the book accomplished our objectives for it.

After the book's initial release and modest successes, I began to think about writing an expanded version that could answer a question left unaddressed in the original, namely, the question of exactly how the laws of the Torah apply to Gentile believers in Jesus. First Fruits of Zion took advantage of the sixth printing in 2009 to create a second edition, which corrected several minor errors, but the main contents of the second edition remained unaltered, and the question remained unresolved.

The 2015, tenth anniversary edition gave me the opportunity to thoroughly revisit the original material, upgrade the writing, and add new material that I have developed since the book was first released. The new version of *Restoration* contains three new chapters of material and an appendix. The new material explains how the Torah applies to Gentile believers in Jesus by exploring New Testament teachings on the subject. Special focus rests on the implications of the apostolic decision to exempt the non-Jewish disciples from circumcision (Acts 15). In the original version of *Restoration*, I passed swiftly over that subject because I did not understand it well. As a result, the book failed to make a clear distinction between Jewish believers and Gentile believers and their respective obligations under the Torah. The new edition has rectified that problem.

Special thanks to Jacob Fronczak and Sheldon Wilson for their input into the fourth edition. Thanks to Boaz Michael and the whole team at First Fruits of Zion. Thanks to the *FFOZ Friends* for making the whole adventure possible.

INTRODUCTION

The Prophetic Return to Torah

This is a book for the disciples of Jesus, both Jews and Gentiles. It's a book about the Torah (also known as "the Law") and how the Torah relates to disciples of Jesus. It's also a book about an ancient prophecy from 3,400 years ago coming true in our own lifetimes—a prophecy of restoration. This prophetic restoration has implications for all disciples of Jesus, both Jews and Gentiles.

Way back then, in the days of the Bible, Moses foresaw the future, and he told us what would happen. The things that he said are happening today. The book of Deuteronomy records his prophecies.

Moses foresaw a dark time of exile for the Jewish people. He saw Israel scattered among the nations, driven from place to place, scorned, mocked, rejected, and persecuted. At every turn, history has proven his words. For nearly two thousand years, the Jewish people have lived in exile. Wandering, bitterly oppressed, hated and reviled, homeless and hapless, a proverb and a taunt among all the people, in hunger, in thirst, and in the lack of all things, scattered from one end of the earth to the other, without rest and without a resting place, with trembling heart, failing eyes and despair of soul, in dread of night and the heat of day, with no assurance of life, so that their lives hung in doubt.

Yet even the darkest and longest nights end with the dawning of a new day. Moses foresaw a time of restoration when Israel's long night of exile would end. The sun would yet rise on Jacob.

Moses said that God would bring the Jewish people back to the land of Israel:

> The LORD your God will restore you from captivity, and have compassion on you, and will gather you again from all the peoples where the LORD your God has scattered you. If your outcasts are at the ends of the earth, from there the LORD your God will gather you, and from there He will bring you back. The LORD your God will bring you into the land which your fathers possessed, and you shall possess it. (Deuteronomy 30:3–5)

In the last half of the nineteenth century, the Jewish people began to return to their ancient homeland. In the middle of the twentieth century, the United Nations partitioned off part of the Holy Land for a Jewish homeland, and the modern State of Israel was born. The ancient prophecy is being fulfilled. God is on the move. He is restoring His people.

But this restoration entails more than just the return of the Jewish people to the promised land. Moses went on to predict that the Jewish people will also return to the Law (Torah). He said, "And you shall again obey the LORD, and observe all His commandments which I command you today" (Deuteronomy 30:8). The commandments of which he speaks are the commandments of God's Law. The Hebrew word for the Law is *Torah*. It's the first five books of the Bible: Genesis, Exodus, Leviticus, Numbers, and Deuteronomy.

TORAH: God's Law, the first five books of the Bible

The rest of the biblical prophets repeated what God had first promised through Moses. Isaiah, Ezekiel, Jeremiah, and all the other prophets made the same predictions about a future restoration of the Jewish people. The prophets all say that when the final redemption comes, the people of Israel will return to the land, and they will return to the Torah.

The people of Israel are still returning to the land. Jewish immigrants arrive in Israel by the thousands every year. The return to Torah has begun as well. Despite the secular agenda of the postmodern world, Jewish people everywhere are rediscovering the Torah. They are turning back to the ancient paths. They are rediscovering the Sabbath, the biblical festivals, and the wealth of Israel's eternal heritage. Modern Judaism calls this phenomenon the *Teshuvah* movement, a Hebrew word meaning "return."

In the last several decades, traditional Judaism has seen significant growth as secular Jews abandon the spiritual emptiness of the postmodern world and return to faith in God. Moreover, thousands of Jews have found their way back to faith with the conviction that Jesus is the Messiah of Israel—and that's a part of the return to Torah, too. These Jewish believers in Jesus refer to themselves as Messianic Jews. Many of them practice Messianic Judaism—a sect of Judaism that teaches that Jesus of Nazareth is the Messiah, the New Testament is true, and the kingdom is at hand.

MESSIANIC JEW: A Jewish believer in Jesus

MESSIANIC JUDAISM: A sect of Judaism that teaches that Jesus of Nazareth is the Messiah, the New Testament is true, and the kingdom is at hand.

One might object that Jews who believe in Jesus are better defined as Christians. That may be true in many respects, but Messianic Jews identify themselves more readily with Judaism and the Jewish people than with the Christian church. The differences between Messianic Judaism and conventional Christianity are sometimes subtle, but at other times, they can be substantial.

Some of the differences involve days of worship and forms of worship. For example, Messianic Jews assemble on Saturday rather than Sunday and their services follow the synagogue model rather than a conventional church service.

Some of the differences are primarily cosmetic. For example, Messianic Jews call Jesus by His Hebrew name, "Yeshua." They prefer the title "Messiah" over and above the Greek-based term "Christ." Both words mean the same thing: "The Anointed One."

YESHUA: The Hebrew name of Jesus

MESSIAH: The Jewish term for Christ

Some of the differences are more profound. They involve theological differences over the role of the Torah, the Jewish people, and biblical eschatology.

The appearance of modern Messianic Judaism indicates that the ancient prophecy of Moses is being fulfilled. Today's Messianic Jews—especially those Messianic Jews living in the land of Israel—are the first fruits of the prophetic restoration that Moses predicted. If we are willing to open our eyes and see it, we will recognize the hand of God at work among His ancient people, restoring Israel and preparing the Jewish people for the revelation of the kingdom.

The coming of the Messiah has drawn near. It's right at the door. The signs are here: Jewish people are returning to the land of Israel; Jewish people are returning to the Torah; Jewish people are returning to the Messiah. They are responding to the prompt and call of God's Spirit, and it is not just Jews who are feeling the tug of that calling.

Around the world, spontaneously and simultaneously, believers in Jesus are rediscovering the Torah. Even Gentile Christians are taking hold of the biblical Sabbath and celebrating the Bible's holy days. They are studying their Bibles in the light of Jewish sources. They are turning to Messianic Judaism for answers about the Bible. Messianic Jewish congregations today fill with "Messianic Gentiles" hungry to learn about Torah and to take hold of the Jewish roots of their faith. Even non-Messianic rabbis have noted the sudden influx of non-Jews coming into their synagogues, full of questions about the Torah.

It seems as if people from all nations are being swept along in this prophetic restoration. Ultimately, this restoration will culminate in the coming of Messiah and the establishment of His kingdom, when all nations will say, "Come, let us go up to the mountain of the LORD, to the house of the God of Jacob, that He may teach us concerning His ways and that we may walk in His paths" (Isaiah 2:3). The Gentiles seeking the Torah today can be considered to be the first fruits of the fulfillment of this prophecy.

All the disciples of Yeshua have an inheritance in the coming kingdom, and in the kingdom, the Torah will be for everyone. In that day, "The Torah will go forth from Zion and the word of the LORD from Jerusalem" (Isaiah 2:3). That's why this book is for both Jews and Gentiles—because the coming restoration is for both Jews and Gentiles.

This book raises questions about the practical implications of that prophetic picture. If God is going to restore the Torah to the disciples of Jesus in the coming kingdom, does that not imply that the Torah has some pertinence to us today? What role does the Torah play in our faith? Has the New Testament canceled it or replaced it? Which commandments should we be keeping? Should disciples of Yeshua observe the Sabbath and the holy days or eat according to the Bible's dietary laws? Is the Torah the same for both Jews and Gentile believers, or is there some distinction? Where do Paul's teachings about the Law fit into the picture? What about the sacrifices and ceremonial laws? Do they need to be restored too? What about the difficult laws of the Torah like stoning adulterers and Sabbath-breakers? These are a few of the questions and objections that should spring to mind when the topic of Old Testament Law comes up among Christians and disciples of Yeshua.

Are we seeing the fulfillment of the prophecy Moses made 3,400 years ago? God is restoring His people by returning the Jewish people to the land of Israel, to the Torah of Moses, and to the Messiah Yeshua. Ultimately, He will restore the whole world. Has the restoration already begun?

CHAPTER ONE

My Journey to Torah

I'm not Jewish. I am a country pastor's son. My parents expected a girl. They already had three boys and two girls. They expected a third girl to balance out the family. Fully anticipating the birth of a daughter, they had already picked out a name for me. I was supposed to be called Sarah Joy. When I was born a male child, they were at a loss for what to name me. According to the story, a day or so after I was born, the LORD individually impressed upon my parents, and on my siblings as well, that my name was to be Daniel Thomas.

THOMAS THE DOUBTER

I go by Daniel, but I have always preferred the Thomas side to the name because I identify more readily with the pragmatic, doubting disciple Thomas than I do with the mystical, vision-seeing prophet Daniel. My doubts fuel my studies. Nevertheless, I am a believer, and I have been a confessing believer in Jesus since the age of four.

I grew up in a small, non-denominational, fundamentalist church that, in later years, came to be affiliated with the Evangelical Free Church of America. The church was called Swan Lake. It sat at the intersection of two country roads in the midst of endless miles of plowed prairie: fields of corn and soybeans as far as the eye could see. The lawn of the church was the only known piece of virgin prairie that remained in that flat land of big sky and wide horizons. The ruts of an old wagon road from pioneer times had left still-visible depressions in the grass crossing the property.

My father led Swan Lake until I was four years old. He set aside full-time ministry in order to take a job that provided a more adequate income on which to raise six children. Yet he continued to be a serious spiritual influence on my life, as he still is today. He is a man of great humility in possession of a great truth: the saving grace of the gospel of Messiah. His greatest gift to me was the impartation of a solid grasp of that truth.

He was only the first in a long series of short-term pastors who came through our tiny rural church. At Swan Lake Evangelical Free Church, we taught the gospel and generally believed ourselves to be the only outpost of true believers in the vicinity. We lived by the Bible—for the most part. While presenting sermons, our pastors often quipped, "Don't just take my word for it. Read the Bible yourself." I did.

As a young teen, I decided to read through the Bible for the first time. When I did, I noticed several glaring inconsistencies between the biblical text and what I thought I knew about the Bible. The words of Jesus were particularly unsettling. He seemed legalistic. He almost never talked about going to heaven when you die. I began to have a sick feeling in my stomach.

Another inconsistency that bothered me involved the biblical Sabbath. I noticed that the Sabbath occurs on the seventh day, Saturday, and the Bible makes nary a mention of a Sunday Sabbath for Christians. Still, I never considered the seventh day as relevant to Christians because, to me, Sabbath and church were synonymous, and church always took place on Sunday. All the same, I knew something was amiss. I felt the clouds of doubt gathering around me.

ACQUIRING A TEACHER

When I was a teenager, I went to Israel to visit my brother Steven, who was studying and teaching at the Institute of Holy Land Studies in Jerusalem (now called Jerusalem University College). While touring Israel, we visited Jerusalem's *Yad V'Shem* Holocaust museum. For the first time, at sixteen years old, the horror of the Holocaust confronted me. I viewed the exhibits with a young history major from the Institute. The history student remarked,

"No people on earth have been persecuted like the Jewish people." I quickly corrected him saying, "Except for the Christians." He laughed—a sound not often heard in *Yad V'Shem*.

The eyes of the victims stared at me across the photographically reproduced barbed-wire fences. I suddenly realized that I stood on the wrong side of the fence. If we Christians were the real people of God, why did the world still target and hate the Jews? Shouldn't we be the ones on whom the forces of evil bend their energy? Instead, we were too often the ones dispensing the evil. Something began to stir within me.

Shortly thereafter, my brother Steven returned from Israel to study toward his PhD in Semitic languages at the University of Wisconsin in Madison. While in Madison, he attended a Seventh Day Baptist Church. He and a fellow student (who also attended the Seventh Day Baptist Church) took it upon themselves to begin to welcome the Sabbath on Friday evenings in the traditional Jewish manner. When my parents and I visited my brother and his wife on a Friday evening, they brought in the Sabbath with the traditional lighting of candles, the bread, the wine, the blessings, and the prayers of the Sabbath table. The richness of the tradition captivated me. My own religious experience, devoid of ritual and ceremony, seemed to pale in comparison with this simple, eloquent expression of faith: the Sabbath. Here was something of substance. I saw the Messiah in every ritual. The quiet, the peace, and the spiritual essence of the Sabbath filled me with a strange nostalgia and a longing I could not explain.

My brother Steven has had a profound influence on me. Years later, when I began to study and teach the Bible, my brother's work in the biblical languages, the biblical text, and biblical geography inspired me to read the Scriptures within a historical, contextual frame of reference. He encouraged me to learn Hebrew, and he taught me how to handle the text responsibly. He tutored me in careful hermeneutics. When I was finishing college, he wrote independent studies for me in Biblical Hebrew, literary criticism, and Hebrew poetry. I studied his coursework for credit to finish my degree. Under his tutelage, I completed a course in Biblical Geography and received an opportunity to study at the Institute of Holy Land Studies (Jerusalem University College) on Mount Zion, Jerusalem, where he served as a faculty member. He taught me about the land of Israel and the Scriptures of Israel. Whenever a passage of the Bible came under consideration, Steve pointed toward context: language, culture, geography, and history. When I wanted to allegorize a passage, he always pointed me back to its literal meaning. He revolutionized my understanding of the Bible. He gave me an interpretive framework for understanding how the different books of the Bible work together—he taught me the priority of Scripture; in other words, which books must be understood first. He showed me how the Torah forms the foundation upon which all subsequent biblical revelation stands. He taught me that the Bible is supposed to make sense and that it actually does make sense. It is not a collection of disconnected mystical sayings and stray proof texts. It is real literature. He taught me that the Good Book really is a good book.

MESSIANIC JUDAISM

A few years before I began studying under my brother, I encountered Messianic Judaism. My wife and I visited a Messianic Jewish congregation. It was a strange, awkward experience. The congregation consisted of a small fellowship—not more than a dozen people gathering on Sabbaths to learn Torah.

Messianic Judaism starts with the assumption that Christianity was originally Jewish. Jesus, the apostles, and all the first disciples were practicing Jews who considered themselves part of Israel and the Jewish people. They did not envision themselves as the authors of a new religion; they considered themselves to be a sect within greater Judaism—a reformation movement inspired by the teachings of Yeshua of Nazareth and by their conviction that He was the long-promised Messiah King. They belonged to the sect of the Nazarenes, a first-century Jewish school of disciples centered on Yeshua. They did not hold Yeshua or the gospel message in antithesis to the Torah of Moses. They upheld the words of Jesus: "Do not think that I came to abolish the Law ..." (Matthew 5:17).

The modern Messianic Jewish movement was born from Christian missionary efforts to evangelize Jews. In the late nineteenth century, the products of this missionary activity—Jewish believers in Jesus—began to take ownership of their faith, eschewing Gentile Christian modes of worship and interpretation and working to establish an authentic Jewish expression of faith. In the 1960s and 1970s, this movement blossomed in the United States among young Jewish Christians of the Baby-Boom generation. Since then it has outgrown its original chrysalis as a Jewish missionary effort and has begun to emerge as an independent sect of Judaism, much as the community of the original apostles did.

Similarly, Messianic Judaism, following in the footsteps of the early Jesus movement, includes a predominant number of Gentile participants. These Gentile Christians have entered the movement seeking a more historically authentic form of Christianity. In that regard, Messianic Judaism is no longer an exclusively Jewish movement (if it ever was), but instead it includes many "Messianic Gentiles" who, while not being Jewish, nevertheless have found a spiritual home in the Messianic synagogue. I was one of those Gentiles.

In one month at the Messianic synagogue, I learned more Bible than I had learned in all my years at church. We learned about the Jewish roots of Christianity. We learned about the Sabbath and the biblical festivals. I began to see Yeshua, the real, biblical Jesus—the Jewish Jesus—and I began to understand Him in His Jewish context. I felt as if my eyes had opened. I felt as if I was reading the Scriptures for the first time.

The thrill of discovery felt exhilarating. At first, I assumed that our family and the few people attending the synagogue with us were the only people in the whole world who understood the Scriptures this way. Then we discovered a ministry called First Fruits of Zion (FFOZ) and realized that we were not alone. The materials of FFOZ came to us like water in a dry and thirsty land.

Torah study was eye-opening, revolutionary, explosive, and thrilling. It was like an antidote to doubt, and it fueled me on to study all the more. My misgivings about the Bible began to vanish. The more I studied the Torah and the Jewishness of Jesus and the early believers, the more the Doubting Thomas side of me diminished.

If you have not yet had the opportunity to learn the Bible from a Messianic Jewish perspective, you will not understand what I mean. Terms like eye-opening, faith-building, and paradigm-shifting all fall short of describing the joy of reading and studying the Scriptures in their Jewish context. Not that this should be surprising. After all, the Bible is a thoroughly Jewish book. How did we Christians ever hope to understand the Bible without understanding its historical context—without understanding the Torah and Judaism?

Imagine a person who has grown up with blurred vision. He assumes that everyone sees the world in the same blurry, hazy, indistinct shapes that he does. He assumes that blurriness is normal. He does not know he is missing anything. Then one day he is given a pair of corrective lenses. Immediately the world takes on sharp definition. He realizes how much he has been missing. Studying the Bible from a Jewish perspective feels a lot like that.

It was a revolutionary journey for me. The whole Messianic Jewish perspective was life-saving because, in many ways, it salvaged my faith—a real restoration.

DANIEL THE JUDAIZER?

I began to study Torah in earnest in the context of traditional Judaism. I immersed myself in the world of traditional Jewish literature. I devoured Torah, Talmud, Midrash and classical Jewish commentary on the Bible. I remember how my heart burned within me as the rabbi expounded on the Torah. In every word he said, in every passage we studied, it seemed the image of Messiah stepped forth in brilliant colors. At times I felt that I would burst from the excitement. I've never felt closer to the Master than when studying Torah in the midst of His people.

I emerged from those years with a passion to bring Torah to my brothers and sisters in Christ. I took positions teaching adult Christian education classes in large evangelical churches. Other teaching opportunities opened, and soon I was teaching in churches and Messianic Jewish congregations as many as four to five times a week. It was through these various teaching opportunities that I received the dubious honor of being dubbed a "Judaizer."

What is a Judaizer?

In the next chapter, we will see that according to the way that many of the church fathers and reformers would define the term, I am a Judaizer. That does not mean that I want to make Christians into Jews. It simply means that I am encouraging Christians to return to what I understand to be the original form of Christianity. I am teaching Christians that God's laws, in one fashion or another, apply to them.

The classic church understands a Judaizer as one who encourages Christians to adopt Jewish practices, such as observance of the Sabbath and the biblical festivals. According to that definition of the word, I'm a Judaizer.

Note that the biblical term "Judaizer" is different. In the Bible, a Judaizer is someone who teaches that a Gentile must undergo conversion to become Jewish and keep the Torah as a Jew. When Peter separated from the Gentile believers in Antioch, he did so under pressure from Jewish believers from Jerusalem who believed that Gentiles were not worthy of table fellowship unless they became Jewish. Paul rejected this idea and accused Peter of Judaizing by capitulating to that opinion: "How is it that you compel the Gentiles to *Judaize*" (Galatians 2:14).

Paul wrote his epistle to the Galatians to refute the Judaizing believers at work within the Galatian community.

CONVENTIONAL DEFINITION OF A JUDAIZER: One who encourages Christians to adopt Jewish practices, such as observance of the Sabbath and the biblical festivals.

BIBLICAL DEFINITION OF A JUDAIZER: One who compels non-Jews to become Jewish and keep the Torah as Jews in order to merit salvation.

According to the biblical definition, I am not a Judaizer. I do not compel non-Jews to become Jewish. Maybe I am a Judaizer by the conventional definition, but I also recognize that the Bible distinguishes between Jews and Gentiles, and according to the Bible, Gentile believers are not required to keep all the same commandments as the Jewish people.

Moreover, I believe that "by grace you have been saved through faith; and that not of yourselves, it is the gift of God; not as a result of works, so that no one may boast" (Ephesians 2:8–9). I do not believe in keeping the Law in order to be saved. I believe in keeping it because I am saved. Nonetheless, that belief makes me, according to the conventional opinions, a Judaizer.

DANIEL THE LEGALIST?

Not only am I a Judaizer, I am a legalist.

How does a person become a legalist? What is a legalist?

Once again, we find a conventional definition of legalism and a theological definition. In conventional usage, a legalist is anyone who believes that he or others should keep a particular law or commandment from the Bible that is no longer practiced in the church. For example, if a pastor were to tell the teenagers in his congregation that they should not get tattoos because Leviticus 19:28 forbids it, that would be regarded as a legalistic interpretation. The young people in his youth group would probably charge him with being a legalist. (I know of a situation where this actually occurred.) I believe that getting a tattoo is wrong, so that makes me a legalist. But I am not a legalist in the biblical sense.

"Legalist" is not a biblical word, but it is a biblical idea. In the Bible, a legalist is essentially the same as a Judaizer. It is someone who teaches that we must keep the commandments of God in order to merit His grace, affection, favor, and ultimately salvation. Surprisingly, the legalists were not the Pharisees; they were believers who taught salvation through works. They were Paul's opponents.

I am not that kind of legalist. I am a big fan of the Apostle Paul's writings. Let me state it again. I believe that "by grace you have been saved through faith; and that not of yourselves, it is the gift of God; not as a result of works, so that no one may boast" (Ephesians 2:8–9). To me, that means that I have no personal merit sufficient to earn God's favor, nor can I generate it. I do not believe in keeping the Law in order to be saved or even to maintain salvation. But I do believe in keeping the Law because I am saved. That belief makes me, according to the conventional definition of the term, a legalist.

CONVENTIONAL DEFINITION OF LEGALIST: One who compels Christians to live by a certain standard or commandment of Scripture that is no longer generally practiced in the church.

THEOLOGICAL DEFINITION OF LEGALIST: One who attempts to earn salvation through obedience to the law.

According to the biblical parameters as expressed in Paul's epistles, I am not a legalist, nor am I a Judaizer. But according to the conventional use of the terminology, I am both. The rest of this book explains why.

DANIEL THE HERETIC?

In some circles, I will be regarded as worse than a legalist and Judaizer; I will be seen as a heretic. According to many Christian authorities, teaching Christians to keep the biblical laws of Torah is heresy. Wow! How does a person become a heretic? Probably by reading books like this one.

Let me encourage you to keep reading anyway. In the study of Torah, the conclusion is sometimes less important than the process of study because the study of Torah is the study of God's Word. As my pastors always told me, "Don't just take my word for it. Read the Bible yourself."

It was good advice. It changed my life.

If, after reading the rest of this book, you do not reach the same (seemingly heretical) conclusions I have, you will nevertheless be better prepared to give an answer when you encounter other "legalists" and "Judaizers" like me.

CHAPTER TWO

The Journey away from Torah

The Jewish people have lived in exile since the age of the apostles. So has the gospel.

THE GOSPEL IN EXILE

The gospel is in exile because, like the Jewish people, it has been removed from context and disconnected from its point of origin. The gospel began in the land of Israel. Like the Jewish people, the gospel suffered Roman persecution and spread out into every nation. Like the Jewish people, the gospel now resides among the nations of the Diaspora.

These years of exile have been productive for both the Jewish people and the gospel. Like the Jewish people in exile, the gospel has flourished. Like the Jewish people in exile, it has entered every nation and every culture on the globe. Like the Jewish people in exile, the gospel has impacted the entire world.

But the time is nigh for the exile to come to an end.

Moses foresaw a time of restoration. He foresaw a time when the people of Israel would return from exile and turn back to the commandments of God. "And you shall again obey the LORD, and observe all His commandments which I command you today" (Deuteronomy 30:8). That restoration requires a return to the gospel of Messiah. Now, at the culmination of the ages, Jewish people are returning to the land. They are returning to the Torah. In a similar way, they are returning to the gospel, and the gospel itself is returning from exile. New Testament scholars are returning the gospel to its Jewish context and reconnecting it with its Jewish origins. Let me explain what I mean.

THE EARLY DAYS

In the days of the apostles, Christianity was not yet a separate religion from Judaism. An honest reading of the New Testament from a Jewish perspective makes it clear that the first-century church never thought of itself as separate and excluded from Judaism. Rather, the early disciples of Yeshua considered themselves to be at the center of the people of Israel. The Jewish disciples never imagined that they were introducing a new religion to replace Judaism. They might have considered themselves to be bringing a restoration within Judaism, but they did not think of themselves as a separate entity.

The writings of the apostles assume the believers to be a sect within the larger religion of Judaism. Jesus was actually a Jewish teacher of Torah. His Hebrew name—that is, His real name—was Yeshua. He kept the Torah, taught the Torah, and lived by the Torah. He taught His disciples to keep the Torah in imitation of Him. He argued with the teachers of other sects of Judaism. He denounced the Sadducees, rebuked the Pharisees, and brought correction to their teachings, but He did not institute a new religion, nor did He cancel the Torah. Instead, He sought to bring restoration to the ancient faith of Abraham, Isaac, and Jacob. He diligently sought after the lost sheep of Israel—those who had turned away from Torah. He affirmed the words of Moses and brought clarification regarding the proper observance of God's Law. His followers, the apostles and the believers, also remained within the parameters of normative, first-century Jewish expression. They met daily in the Temple. They congregated in synagogues. They proclaimed the Scriptures of Israel. They kept the biblical festivals, the Sabbaths, the dietary laws, and the whole of Torah as best they were able. They were all Jews.

GENTILE INCLUSION

When non-Jews began to enter the faith through the ministry of Paul of Tarsus, they too congregated in synagogues and embraced the standards of Judaism. They understood themselves to be "grafted in" to the nation of Israel and made citizens of the larger "commonwealth of Israel." They considered themselves to be co-heirs of the kingdom and co-religionists with the Jewish people.

The apostles disagreed over their status. Should they be required to become Jewish and keep the whole Torah as Jews, or was it sufficient for them to remain as non-Jews and observe only those commandments that applied to the strangers within Israel?[1] Paul, the apostle to the Gentiles, argued fiercely for their inclusion as Gentiles. He argued that the Gentiles need not be "under the law" (i.e., Jewish), in order to be saved. He argued that they were saved by grace, not by the "works of the Law" (i.e., becoming Jewish). Not everyone agreed with his ideas.

The apostles met to discuss the question, and they decided to adopt the latter course. They ruled that ritual conversion (i.e., "circumcision") was not required of the Gentile disciples. Neither were they required to forsake their ethnic identity and become Jewish. Yet their faith was the faith of Israel, placed in the Messiah of Israel, and they henceforth practiced the religion of Israel. They observed the laws of the Torah that applied to them as Gentiles among the people of Israel. They congregated with the Jewish people and participated in the life of Torah as God-fearers and sojourners within the nation.

The Jewish believers, for their part, continued to fulfill all the Torah's requirements, just as Yeshua had instructed. And just as the apostles had envisioned, synagogues initially welcomed the Gentile believers into their communities.

This idyllic coexistence, however, was not to last.

The inclusion of Gentiles did not go smoothly. Gentiles often found themselves unwelcome in the local synagogue. Their presence created friction between the Jewish believers and the rest of the Jewish community. As a result, the Gentile believers felt disenfranchised from both the Gentile world and the Jewish world.

DRAMATIC EVENTS

The end of the book of Acts leaves us with the impression that the Yeshua movement was still a part of wider Judaism, still a sect within the wider Jewish people.[2] We catch a final glimpse from around the year 62 CE. Paul was a prisoner in the city of Rome, ministering to the believers in Rome. That same year, the Sadducees murdered James the brother of the Master, throwing him down from the parapet of the Temple. Two years later, the wicked Emperor Nero launched a horrific persecution against the believers, falsely blaming them for the fire of Rome. The Romans crucified Simon Peter in a Roman Circus, and, a short while later, they condemned Paul to beheading. Later that year, Nero sent his dreaded legions, under the famous General Vespasian, to put down a revolt in Judea. Suddenly, Jews were regarded as enemies of the state, and anyone associated with Jews fell under suspicion.

Our brothers and sisters in Jerusalem heeded the words of the Master. He had forewarned them, saying:

> When you see Jerusalem surrounded by armies, then recognize that her desolation is near. Then those who are in Judea must flee to the mountains, and those who are in the midst of the city must leave, and those who are in the country must not enter the city; because these are days of vengeance, so that all things which are written will be fulfilled. (Luke 21:20–22)

The armies came and the believers fled east across the Jordan River. The Roman legions devastated the Galilee, destroyed Judea, decimated the city of Jerusalem, and burned the Temple. They conducted a massacre. Those who survived were led away into captivity and exile. In one sense, the gospel went into exile with them, scattered among the nations.

GUILT BY ASSOCIATION

The Jewish War gave rise to the politics of anti-Semitism. Jews in the Diaspora became objects of derision, open persecution, and brutality. The war against the Jews further estranged the Gentile disciples of Yeshua.

Imagine a Gentile believer living in the Roman colony of Philippi attending a Jewish worship service on the Jewish day of worship and keeping Jewish rituals when suddenly his nation goes to war with the Jews. Previously he might have been known simply as "Tony the Believer" from Philippi. Subsequent to the revolt his neighbors began to refer to him as "Tony the Jew-lover, enemy of the state" from Philippi, or even just "Tony the Jew."

Emperor Vespasian followed up the Jewish War by imposing a heavy, punitive annual tax upon all Jewish households in the empire. He determined Jewish households as those who worshiped after the Jewish manner. With the addition of the *Fiscus Judaicus* tax, Gentile believers had financial, political, and cultural incentives to distance themselves from Judaism.

EXPULSION FROM THE SYNAGOGUE

Shortly after the Jewish War and the destruction of Jerusalem, synagogues throughout the world introduced a new benediction in the daily liturgies. The new prayer formulated a curse against sectarians—including the believers in Yeshua.[3] The synagogue authorities expelled worshipers who would not pray the curse. Thus the Jewish and Gentile believers both found themselves expelled from the Jewish assembly. The Master had foreseen this. He warned His disciples that "they will make you outcasts from the synagogue" (John 16:2).

Excommunication from the synagogue felt deeply offensive to the believers. It created sharp animosity against Jews (even among Jewish believers), who were already none too popular throughout the empire. What is worse, the expulsion left believers with no place to assemble on the Sabbath, or to assemble at all.

THE DOMITIAN PERSECUTION

The idolatrous Roman world resented the non-Jewish disciples of Yeshua because they seemed in all respects to be Jewish. Near the end of the century, a new emperor, Domitian, the son of Vespasian, fearing another Jewish revolt, unleashed a series of new persecutions against the believers—again because of their Jewish association. In that wave of persecutions, John, the last apostle, went to his exile on the Isle of Patmos.

Put yourself in the sandals of the average Jewish believer. The local synagogue will not tolerate your presence, and the Roman world has targeted you for persecution. Your allegiance to Judaism wears thin in the face of persecution from both worlds.

Put yourself in the sandals of the average non-Jewish believer. On the one hand, the synagogue has thrown you and your family out because you are offensive to Judaism. On the other hand you have seen your friends and family imprisoned, even exiled or killed, because they are identified with the Jewish religion. You are guilty by association with a religion that does not want you associating with them.

THE SECOND CENTURY

By the time the second century began, anti-Jewish sentiment was so high in the church that most Gentile disciples of Yeshua no longer wanted to be identified with Jews at all. The first-century believers were long dead and gone. A new generation had been raised to view Jews and even Jewishness as the antithesis of Christianity. The new Christian attitude toward Judaism was not unlike the bitter hostility many Protestants hold for Catholics. It fills some deep psychological need to define oneself against something. That "something" is often one's parents, which is what Catholics were to Protestants—and what Judaism was to Christianity.

Gentile Christians decided that the Christian church had replaced the Jews as the true Israel of God. Christians were now the true people of God; Jews were accursed and consigned to everlasting damnation.

THE BAR KOCHBA REVOLT

This new generation lived through the Second Jewish War. In the fourth decade of the second century, the Jews of Judea revolted against Rome again, this time during the days of the Emperor

Hadrian. They banded together under the leadership of the rebel warrior Shimon Bar Kochba. Rabbi Akiva declared him to be messiah. All of Bar Kochba's men were told that they must swear allegiance to his messiahship, even proving their allegiance by maiming themselves for him.

The remaining Jewish believers in Judea refused to cast their allegiance behind the false messiah. Early sources suggest that Bar Kochba and his men massacred them.

Bar Kochba was not the messiah. Rome crushed his rebellion. The Jewish people again suffered under imperial persecution. The Talmud calls it the age of the great persecution. In those days, Emperor Hadrian issued laws declaring it illegal to keep the Sabbath, to ordain rabbis, and to practice Judaism. Believers could be arrested for keeping the laws of Torah. Any who did remain faithful to the Torah faced the same consequences as the Jewish people. Rome made no distinction between Jews and Gentile believers practicing the Jewish faith. To survive, it became necessary for Gentile believers to further disassociate from Judaism.

Paul's compiled letters, when read outside their original context, provided ample justification for that disassociation. The emerging Christian movement read Paul's arguments for the inclusion of Gentiles in the kingdom backward to imply the exclusion of Torah.

THE CHURCH FATHERS

We call the leaders of the generation of Gentile Christians who lived through the second Jewish revolt the church fathers. They were godly men doing the best they could with the understanding they had. Unfortunately, they had only misunderstandings when it came to Torah and the Jewish people. One of the earliest church fathers, Ignatius the bishop of Antioch, wrote an epistle to the congregations of Asia (where Paul and John had lived and served several decades earlier). He said to them:

> Let us therefore no longer keep the Sabbath after the Jewish manner, and rejoice in days of idleness ... But let every one of you keep the Sabbath in a spiritual manner ... not in relaxation, not in eating things prepared the day

> before, not in finding delight in dancing and clapping which have no sense in them.[4]

What did he mean? Why did he have to prohibit second-century Christians from keeping the Sabbath? He had to prohibit them because, despite all the adversity, second-century Christians in Asia Minor were still keeping Sabbath.

In the same era, men like the author of the so-called *Epistle of Barnabas* arose. *Barnabas* is a second-century document that corrupts and misuses earlier teachings inherited from Jewish believers. It attempts to prove that the Torah was never meant to be taken literally. The final redactor of the pseudo-epistle describes the Jews as wretched men deluded by an evil angel (that is, the God of the Hebrew Scriptures) and abandoned by God. In the *Epistle of Barnabas*, the laws of Torah are allegorized and Judaism is condemned. The early church accepted the *Epistle of Barnabas* as an authentic and worthy epistle, and they publicly read it along with other works of the New Testament.

The second century also gave us the first record of Gentile Christians proselytizing Jews. A famous Christian-Jewish dialogue exists in the form of a polemic between a Hellenist Jew named Trypho and the church father Justin Martyr. *Dialogue with Trypho* demonstrates how far the second-century Christians had already divorced themselves from Judaism and Torah. Justin Martyr explained to Trypho (and all the Jews) that God gave the Torah to the Jews as a punishment for their exceptional wickedness and because of His special hatred for the Jewish people. He said, "We, too, would observe your circumcision of the flesh, your Sabbath days and in a word all your festivals, if we were not aware of the reason why they were imposed upon you, namely, because of your sins and your hardness of heart." Yet even Justin Martyr admitted that, in his day (circa 150 CE), many Jewish believers still practiced the laws of Torah. These "weak-minded" brothers, he reluctantly conceded, were still saved, despite their insistence on observing the laws of Moses.[5]

At the same time that men such as Ignatius and Justin Martyr held sway over the developing church, the Christians in Rome witnessed the arrival of the great heretic Marcion. He came sweeping through the church with a new doctrine. He taught that the Jesus of the New Testament had defeated and unseated the evil god of the Jews. Therefore, the Hebrew Scriptures (what we call the Old Testament) and any Jewish relics in the Christian faith needed to be expelled. He compiled the first version of the "New Testament." Marcion's Bible consisted of portions of the book of Luke and ten of Paul's epistles, which he edited to remove what he termed as "Jewish corruptions." He discarded the rest of the books of the apostles, as well as the entire Old Testament, on the basis of their Jewishness.

Marcion's anti-Jewish, anti-Torah version of Christianity caught on quickly. Though the Roman church denounced him as a heretic in 144 CE, Marcionite churches, bishops, and communities sprang up throughout the Roman Empire. Tertullian compared the Marcionites to "swarms of wasps building combs in imitation of the bees."[6] Marcion's teachings were popular and influential; they remained deeply rooted—even after the church fathers denounced him for his heresies.

RESURRECTION SUNDAY

By the early second century, Christians already observed the first day of the week as "the Lord's Day," but that observance had not yet eclipsed the Sabbath. Initially, believers in Yeshua observed the Sabbath, and then gathered together for a special commemorative meal on Saturday night, after the Sabbath had concluded and the first day of the week had begun.

Meanwhile an annual remembrance of the resurrection of Messiah had emerged in Roman Christian practice. It occurred every year on the Sunday that followed Passover. The Roman Christians celebrated Passover only as a one-day commemoration of the resurrection. Passover Sunday replaced the observance of Passover and the seven-day Festival of Unleavened Bread.

The Roman bishop wanted Christians everywhere to follow the new custom. He ordered believers to quit reckoning Passover by the traditional Jewish method and to only keep this annual resurrection festival. The innovation set off a great controversy because the churches of Asia Minor (the congregations of Paul and John) did not want to capitulate. They wanted to keep Passover as they had learned it from the apostles. In the end the authority of Rome prevailed.

Fallout from the controversy elevated the observance of the first day of the week while diminishing or eliminating the observance of the Jewish (biblical) holy days. Christianity took up the practice of fasting on the Sabbath and rejoicing on Sunday as a weekly celebration of the resurrection of Jesus.

CONSTANTINE AND NICEA

By the time Constantine converted to Christianity and declared it the official state religion, most of the Jewish elements were gone. Except for holdout sects of Jewish believers like the Nazarenes and the Ebionites, the observance of Torah had been largely eliminated from the faith. Constantine made the divorce from Judaism final with the Council of Nicea (325 CE). He said, "Let us have nothing in common with the detestable Jewish rabble."[7] The decisions made at Nicea defined the course the church would take henceforth. Later church councils followed suit, introducing new legislation to forbid Christians from observing Torah. The Council of Antioch (341 CE) prohibited Christians from celebrating Passover with the Jews, while the Council of Laodicea (363 CE) forbade Christians from observing the Sabbath. The edicts of these various councils make it clear that many believers still observed the Torah and practiced Judaism, even in the fourth century.

CHRYSOSTOM

In the late fourth century, John Chrysostom delivered a series of sermons in Antioch against the Jews and against the Judaizers among the Christians. The church fathers applied the term "Judaizer" to anyone who practiced the laws of Torah. Chrysostom's sermons contained an abundance of hateful, anti-Jewish venom. He singled out the observance of Torah as a disease in Christianity:

> What is this disease? The festivals of the pitiful and miserable Jews are soon to march upon us one after the other and in quick succession: the Feast of Trumpets, the Feast of Tabernacles, the fasts [i.e., the Day of Atonement].

> There are many in our ranks who say they think as we do. Yet some of these are going to watch the festivals and others will join the Jews in keeping their feasts and observing their fasts. I wish to drive this perverse custom from the church right now … But now that the Jewish festivals are close by and at the very door, if I should fail to cure those who are sick with the Judaizing disease … [they] may partake in the Jews' transgressions."[8]

Chrysostom went on to denounce Christians who participated in the festivals, the Sabbath, and the dietary laws. He rebuked them for attending the synagogue. He delivered eight consecutive sermons on the subject, ample testimony that even in the fourth century, many believers still observed the Torah and remained in the orbit of the synagogue. In the end, the will of the church prevailed, and the divorce between Christianity and Judaism was completed.

These things had been foreseen. The Master warned His disciples that, in the troubled times to come, "Many will fall away … False prophets will arise and will mislead many. Because lawlessness is increased" (Matthew 24:10–12). Paul had warned the Ephesian elders that "after my departure savage wolves will come in among you, not sparing the flock; and from among your own selves men will arise, speaking perverse things, to draw away the disciples after them" (Acts 20:19–30). In writing to the Thessalonians, he warned them of an apostasy to come, an apostasy of Torahlessness: "Let no one in any way deceive you, for it will not come unless the apostasy comes first … For the mystery of lawlessness is already at work" (2 Thessalonians 2:3, 7).

THE DARK AGES

The church stumbled blindly into the Dark Ages and turned violent toward the Jewish people. Christians burned synagogues and holy books and put whole communities to death. Jewish men and women endured torture and martyrdom—all in the name of Christ. The spilled blood of the Jewish people stains the pages of church history.

The church tightened her grip on her own people by forbidding laity from possessing a copy of the Scriptures. The Holy Book was forbidden. A person caught with a copy of the Scriptures could be sentenced to death. Like the Jewish people, the gospel seemed truly lost in exile, lost among the nations.

THE REFORMATION

Almost five hundred years ago, the return from exile began. Imagine yourself in Germany, as a German Christian, in the year 1517. When you attend church, you go into a beautiful building with high stone spires and vaulted ceilings, stained glass and marble, candlelit masses, monks chanting in Latin, a priest to hear your confession, another priest to sing the mass, incense and votives, Mary, the baby Jesus, Saint Peter, Saint Paul, Saint Ann, the Holy Father in Rome. The Mass is inspiring. The architecture is captivating. The liturgy is lofty, high, and holy. We have come a long way from the simple, first-century sect of Judaism that proclaimed the man from Nazareth to be resurrected from the dead.

But there are some things amiss here. The Mass proclaiming the mystery of Christ is beautiful—but you can't understand a word of it, unless you have a university education and can speak Latin, which isn't likely. The pictures of the Madonna, the Christ Child, Saint Peter, and Saint Paul are as much of the Scripture as you are likely to really know because there is no Bible available for the common person. Bibles are all written in Latin, and the church forbids the laity from possessing a copy.

When you go to the priest to say your confession, he might charge you a fee for the service. You are expected to pay for forgiveness. For an extra donation you can buy grace for dead relatives to release them from torment faster. Relief sculptures mocking and ridiculing the Jewish people are carved into the architecture of the church. That is what you know about Jews. Utter contempt and utter disdain.

But listen to that pounding sound.

Outside the door, someone is standing on a ladder. He is nailing something to the door. It is the year 1517, the year Martin Luther, a disillusioned Augustine monk from the Black Monastery in Erfert, nailed his Ninety-five Theses to the church door in Wittenberg.

If you take the time to read his Ninety-five Theses, it may surprise you to discover how benign it is. It does not contain a list of radical reforms that Luther sought to impose on the church. It makes no statement against the authority of the papacy or Rome. It does not indict the church for the adoration of images or the worship of saints. It does not call into question the theology of worshiping Mary as the mother of God. It only presents a sustained argument against the selling of indulgences—that is, charging people for grace and forgiveness.

But it was enough. Someone had dared to question the authority of the church to impose its own doctrines against the Scripture. Someone had dared to say, "Hey, wait a second. That's not in the Bible. That's not part of the original Christian faith."

Once that point had been made, no one could stop the inevitable. Thanks to Gutenberg's printing press, Bibles began appearing in common languages so that anyone who wanted to could read what was written. The average person could read and understand the stories in the Gospels, the words of the Master, the words of Paul, the whole of the Scriptures. We call this era the Protestant Reformation.

Did Luther's Reformation go far enough? Clearly the myriad daughter denominations of the Protestant Reformation do not think so. Each subsequent Protestant movement has contributed its own set of further reforms. Ostensibly, each reform is an attempt to reach further back to the original first-century church of Yeshua and His disciples.

The effort to return to the first-century church is praiseworthy. It reflects our desire to conform our lives and religious expression to the authority of the New Testament. The reformers had good motives. Their methodology, however, was flawed. An important piece of the puzzle was missing.

What the various Protestant reformers failed to recognize about the New Testament church is that it was Jewish. The church was a part of first-century Judaism. Yeshua, the disciples, the first believers, the worship system, the Scriptures, the interpretation of the Scriptures, the teaching, the vernacular, and even the concepts of faith and grace, Messiah and God—all of these were patently Jewish. Any attempt at church reformation—any attempt to return to the original New Testament church—falls short as long as it refuses to acknowledge the essential Jewishness of our faith.

THE RADICAL REFORMATION

Why did the Protestant Reformation stop where it did? If it was really all about throwing out unbiblical church traditions that had tainted Christianity, why did it retain the Roman calendar and the theologies of the church councils? Why do Protestant churches still call Sunday the Sabbath and eat ham on Easter instead of observing the Sabbath and eating unleavened bread on Passover?

During Luther's lifetime, hopes were high within the Jewish community that the Protestant Reformation would put a stop to Christian persecution of the Jewish people. In fact, the opposite happened. Martin Luther issued an encyclical called *Against the Sabbath Keepers* and another one called *Against the Judaizers.* He admonished Protestant Christians for keeping Sabbath and adopting Jewish customs. In 1543, Luther published *On the Jews and Their Lies,* a tract in which he advocated burning down synagogues in every town and forcing Jews to convert or die.

What was the reason for his rage against the Jewish community? Luther felt disappointed that the Jews did not embrace Protestant Christianity. He had assumed that, once the Jewish people realized that they did not need to become Catholic, they would share his enthusiasm for Protestant Christianity and convert en masse. When they did not respond with mass conversions, he turned against them.

But another development within Luther's own movement contributed to his vitriolic attacks against the Jews. Protestants were reading their Bibles and concluding that authentic, biblical Christianity was Jewish. It's called the "Radical Reformation." Radical Reformation Protestants were returning to Jewish practices, returning to Torah, keeping Sabbath, and observing the festivals. Luther and the Protestant reformers scrambled to stop the Judaization of the Protestant movement.

The Renaissance Age boasted a strong Jewish Roots movement. As early as 1538, just twenty-one years after the Wittenberg door incident, Oswald Dlaidt and Andreas Fischer launched a radical return to Sabbatarianism from within the Anabaptist church of Moravia. Fischer translated synagogue liturgy out of the Hebrew for use in services and even went so far as to write a Christian Siddur, essentially a translation of the Jewish prayer book. For the first time since the Apostolic Era, believers were praying the ancient blessings before eating, they were offering thanks after meals according to the Jewish tradition, and they were praying the basic prayers of the Jewish expression. In response to the Moravian Reformers, Luther wrote *Against the Sabbath Keepers*, a tract condemning Sabbath observance for Christians. Stiff resistance from Luther and persecution from the larger Protestant world snuffed out the Moravian Torah movement.

A reformer by the name of Paul Fagius gave a historical interpretation of the New Testament by explaining the Lord's Supper in the context of Passover and the sayings of Yeshua in the context of rabbinic literature. Luther and his associates labeled him a Judaizer. For Luther and his followers, refuting the Radical Reformation became synonymous with rejecting Judaizers. The reformation was spinning out of control and, in some places, rapidly returning to Jewish form and practice.

Wherever the Bible was read without theological manipulation, believers were returning to Torah. Nevertheless, the anti-Jewish faction prevailed. The return to Torah stalled. The gospel would remain in exile. The time was not yet ripe. Several more centuries would pass before the momentum returned.

POST-HOLOCAUST SCHOLARSHIP

From 1938 to 1945, the Jewish people endured a seven-year great tribulation—a culmination of the horrors of exile. The long years of persecution reached a demonic crescendo. Blackness. Utter despair. Ruin in the face of naked evil. Six million dead. Yet the people of Israel lived.

As the world emerged from the travails of World War II, stories of the Holocaust began to circulate. Slowly, the realization sank in. Christians began to understand what had happened. Many theologians and churchmen were abashed to realize that the religious prejudices and bigotry etched into Christian theology had contributed to the greatest human travesty of all time.

Though he was a self-proclaimed pagan, Hitler justified the genocide by pointing to Christian writings and Christian history. He even quoted Luther. Scholars, historians, and theologians have filled whole libraries with books demonstrating how Hitler's "Final Solution" put Luther's ideas into action.

Ashamed and mortified, Christian thinkers and theologians began to publicly swear off anti-Semitism. As a part of that process, they re-examined old church theologies that had allowed for and even encouraged the historic brutalization of the Jewish people. Bible scholars began to reexamine the assumption that the church had replaced the Jewish people. They also reexamined the assumption that Jews are cursed by God and enemies of Christ. This process initiated a renaissance in Christian thought and theology. A new breed of scholars emerged who were willing to examine the origins of Christianity in light of Jewish sources. We are only now beginning to reap the harvest of post-Holocaust New Testament studies.

DEAD SEA SCROLLS AND THE STATE OF ISRAEL

At the same time, two other remarkable events added momentum to the return to biblical Christianity. Sometime in late 1946 or early 1947, Muhammed edh-Dhib ("The Wolf") and two of his cousins from the Ta'amirah Bedouin tribe were seeking a stray goat when they discovered the mouth to a cave near the Dead Sea. Throwing a stone into the cave, they heard the sound of breaking pottery inside. They later returned to the cave and discovered several clay jars. Three of them contained ancient scrolls, including scrolls of the Prophet Isaiah. At the time, the boys did not understand the value of their find.

They had discovered what would come to be called the Dead Sea Scrolls. The Dead Sea Scrolls are an ancient library of biblical and Jewish religious literature dating from the days of the apostles. They have revolutionized the way we understand first-century Judaism and the origins of Christianity.

In March of 1947, these Bedouin boys sold the scrolls to Kahil Iskander Shahin, a shoemaker in Bethlehem, presumably so that he might utilize the parchment in his trade. Kahil recognized that the documents were ancient and perhaps valuable. He sold four of them to Mar Athanasius Samuel of St. Mark's Monastery in Jerusalem. Professor Eleazar Sukenik of Hebrew University was allowed to see the scrolls and attempted to purchase them, but Mar Samuel did not want to sell the scrolls to the professor.

Sukenik disguised himself and made a secret trip to Arab Bethlehem to pay a visit to Kahil the shoemaker. On November 29, 1947, he purchased the remaining scrolls, one of which was a scroll of the Prophet Isaiah. Coincidentally, November 29, 1947, is the day the United Nations voted to partition Palestine and allow Israel statehood. On the same day, the ancient prophecies of Isaiah and the ancient land of Israel were returned to Jewish hands. These two seemingly unrelated events have launched a revolution in the way we understand our faith and the way we understand the Bible.

The Jewish return to the land of Israel and reestablishment of a Jewish state came as a fulfillment of biblical prophecy. After those two events, it was no longer possible for Christians to dismiss the Jewish people. The ancient prophecies concerning Israel were coming true. Christian thinkers and theologians needed to reconsider the Israel question.

THE MODERN MESSIANIC JEWISH MOVEMENT

The modern-day Messianic Jewish movement has been fueled by these events. The fruit of post-Holocaust scholarship, the enthusiasm over the formation of the State of Israel and Jewish nationalism, and the discovery of the Dead Sea Scrolls have all combined to spark a complete renaissance in the way that early Christianity is studied and understood. Through the work of this new breed of New Testament scholars, we are now able to read and understand the gospel in its Jewish context for the first time since the days of the apostles. The followers of Yeshua are returning to the ways of Torah. Jewish believers are taking back their inheritance. Gentile believers are uncovering the original shape and form of the faith. We see a prophetic reawakening, coinciding with the return of the Jewish people to their ancient homeland.

Coinciding with all these developments, Messianic Judaism emerged. Messianic Judaism began in the nineteenth century as a small, obscure movement pioneered by a handful of isolated Jewish believers in Yeshua who refused to renounce their Jewish identity. It took root in Israel around the time of the War for Independence, and it blossomed in America after the Six-Day War. Secularized Jewish youth in America picked it up and ran with it. Since then, the Messianic Jewish movement has gained momentum and spread across the world. Building on the scholarship of post-Holocaust New Testament scholars, Messianic Jews realized that they had something valuable to bring to the church. Gentile Christians from all denominations began to look to Messianic Jews for teaching.

That's the story of how the disciples of Yeshua lost the Torah of Moses, and how we are finding it again. The long exile of the Jewish people is at its end. The final redemption is just around the corner. In the same way, the long exile of the gospel is at an end. Just as the Jewish people are returning to their native soil, we are returning the gospel to its original matrix in Judaism and the Torah of Moses.

More than three thousand years ago, Moses foresaw the time of restoration. "And you shall again obey the LORD, and observe all His commandments which I command you today" (Deuteronomy 30:8).

CHAPTER THREE

What Is the Torah?

The Torah is the Law of Moses. Specifically, the Torah consists of the books of Genesis, Exodus, Leviticus, Numbers, and Deuteronomy. This is the "Law" that Paul often spoke of in his epistles. Paul used the Greek word *nomos* to translate the Hebrew word *torah*. The word *nomos* means "law," but the Torah is more than just law. It is more than just a legal code.

Paul wrote in Greek, but the concepts he was communicating came from the world of Hebrew thought. His concepts came from the Hebrew Scriptures and the Hebrew religion: Judaism. Although the Greek word *nomos* means "law," its Hebrew equivalent, *torah*, is considerably broader.

BOWS AND ARROWS

Torah comes from the Hebrew verb *yarah*, "to cast, throw, shoot." This same Hebrew root is also used as an archery term meaning "to take aim, to shoot," referencing the practice of shooting an arrow in order to hit a target. The essence of this word then is "to hit the mark." The Torah is God's aim for us.

The opposite of *torah* is *chata*, which means "to miss the mark." *Chata* is the word translated as "sin" in our Bibles. Paul tells us that all have sinned and fallen short of the mark.[9] Do you see the picture? The Torah is the target at which we aim our arrow. When our shot misses and falls short of the target, we have sinned. Sin is missing the mark of the Torah.

When my children were small, my sons and I tried taking up archery. We purchased three bows and a few quivers full of arrows and set to work puncturing an old crib mattress that we set up as a target in our backyard. After launching several volleys of arrows, I realized that I am a terrible "sinner." Shot after shot completely missed the target. If the definition of sin is to be understood as "missing the mark," then, in terms of archery, I am hopelessly sinful.

After I buried several arrows into the planks of our next-door neighbor's wooden fence, my wife forbade me from shooting in the backyard. Like Paul in his epistle to Timothy, I can claim to be among the worst of sinners, in regard to archery and in regard to Torah. In regard to archery, I can't even hit the target, much less a bull's-eye. In regard to Torah I have a heart prone toward sin. I am a mark-misser.

Torah is the mark for which we are to aim. The Torah is God's standard of righteousness. Sin is our failure to hit that mark. And we all fail to hit the mark. "The Torah of the LORD is perfect" (Psalm 19:7), but we are not. "All have sinned and fall short of the glory of God" (Romans 3:23). The Bible calls it "sin" when a person does "any of the things which the LORD has commanded not to be done" (Leviticus 4:2). The Apostle John described it in no uncertain terms: "Everyone who practices sin also practices lawlessness; and sin is lawlessness" (1 John 3:4). Sin, properly defined, is transgression of Torah. We all miss the target. We all sin.

THE END OF THE TORAH

There is a point at which the Torah aims. The bull's-eye of Torah, the careful aim (*yarah*) of Torah, is the perfect Messiah. This is why Paul wrote in his epistle to the Romans, "Messiah is the end of the Torah" (Romans 10:4).

Traditional Christian interpretation reflects a misunderstanding of Paul's words to mean that Messiah is the cancellation of the Torah. The Greek of Romans 10:4 is better understood to mean that Messiah is the "goal" of the Torah. The Greek word *telos*, which our English Bibles translate as "end," is the same word we use in English words such as telephone, television and telescope. *Telos* implies arrival at a goal. The sound of one's voice on the telephone arrives at the goal of the telephone on the other end. This reading fits the context of Romans 10:4 as well. Messiah is the destination at which the journey of Torah arrives. In his epistle to the Galatians Paul writes, "The Torah has become our tutor to lead us to Messiah" (Galatians 3:24). Is Messiah to be understood as the ending of the Torah then? No. He is the end, but not the ending. He is the goal of the Torah, but not the termination of it. In fact, He Himself said, "Do not think that I came to abolish the Torah" (Matthew 5:17).

THE INSTRUCTIONS

The Hebrew archery term *yarah* can also mean "teaching." Torah means instruction and teaching. Torah is the revelation of God's direction, instruction, teaching, and guidance. It is like God's instruction manual for life. We do not function to our fullest potential without the instructions. The Ten Commandments, for example, are one part of the instruction manual for human life.

ALL SCRIPTURE IS TORAH

When we speak of the Law (or Torah), we should immediately think in terms of Genesis, Exodus, Leviticus, Numbers, and Deuteronomy. Those are the books of Moses. But Torah is not limited to the five books of Moses. As we learned above, Torah does not just mean "law," it also means "teaching." Genesis, Exodus, Leviticus, Numbers, and Deuteronomy are the teaching of Moses, the Torah of Moses. But in a broader sense, all Scripture is God-breathed and built upon the revelation of Torah. Therefore, when the rabbis spoke of the Torah, they generally included all the Scriptures in the term. The Psalms and the Prophets, and even the little scrolls of Esther and the book of Ruth, are all considered parts of the Torah of Israel. That is why Paul sometimes said, "It is written in the Law," and then quoted from Psalms.[10] The Master Himself did the same thing.[11] In one sense, the entire Old Testament is Torah.

For believers in Yeshua, the Torah is broader yet. The Gospels, Paul's writings, the other epistles, and the Revelation of John are also Torah. The entire Bible is God's teaching built upon the Torah of Moses.

In traditional Judaism, even the rabbis' extended teachings came to be termed "Torah." The oral traditions, customs, and law, including the Talmud and other later writings, are regarded as additional members of the extended family of Torah. They all teach, in one form or another, and they are all based upon the five books of Moses.

For the purposes of this book, when I speak of the Torah, I am speaking of the formal Torah in its narrowest sense—the five books of Moses: specifically Genesis, Exodus, Leviticus, Numbers, and Deuteronomy.

THE TORAH IS NOT THE OLD COVENANT

The Torah is covenantal.

A covenant is a contract specifying terms and conditions incumbent upon both parties. It is a list of obligations. But more than a simple agreement, a covenant is the defining of a relationship between two parties. Technically, Torah is not one single covenant. It contains several different covenants. Paul refers to the covenants in the Torah as the "covenants of promise."[12] The Torah contains the covenant God made with Noah.[13] It contains the covenants He made with Abraham, Isaac, and Jacob. It contains the covenant He made with the Jewish people at Mount Sinai. It contains the covenant He made with the house of Aaron and the descendants of Phinehas the priest.[14] It contains the covenant God made with Israel by the Jordan River, and it contains the definition of the "new covenant." Therefore, it is not quite correct to think of the Torah as the "old covenant." Rather, the Torah contains many covenants.

On the other hand, it is fair to consider the laws of Torah as part of the covenant between God and the Jewish people because when Israel entered the covenant at Mount Sinai, the people agreed to keep His laws. The Torah's laws are the terms of the covenant between God and the Jewish people. The Bible refers to the Torah as the book of the covenant.[15] Jewish people observe the laws of the Torah as a matter of covenant fidelity.

The covenant God made with Israel at Mount Sinai is a legally binding agreement between God and His people Israel. In 2 Corinthians 3:14 Paul referred to the Torah of Moses as the old covenant so long as a person reads it without the revelation of Messiah. He said that, once we are in Messiah, the veil is "removed." The

Torah remains, but the veil concealing Messiah within it is removed. Similarly, the book of Hebrews quotes the Prophet Jeremiah to prove that, in the new covenant, the Torah will be written upon human hearts:

> For this is the covenant that I will make with the house of Israel after those days, says the LORD: I will put My Torah into their minds, and I will write them on their hearts. (Hebrews 8:10, quoting Jeremiah 31:33)

In that regard, it is not quite correct to equate the Torah and the "old covenant" because the Torah is part of the new covenant, too. Nevertheless, it is correct to think of the Torah as God's covenant with Israel. According to Jeremiah, Paul, and the writer of Hebrews, the newness or oldness of the covenant depends on where one stands in regard to Messiah.

OLD COVENANT: The Torah without revelation of Messiah.

NEW COVENANT: The writing of the Torah on human hearts through the revelation of Messiah.

THE WEDDING VOWS

Covenants are not something we generally encounter in the modern world. One form of covenant we still practice, however, is the marriage covenant. The Torah is like a marriage covenant between God and Israel.

The romance began while Israel was still in Egypt. The LORD declared to Israel, "I will take you for My people, and I will be your God" (Exodus 6:7). This expression sounds close to an ancient legal formulation from the sphere of marriage. In ancient Near East marriages, the groom declared, "You will be my wife and I will be your husband." In a sense, God declared His intention to marry the people of Israel.

The people of Israel are the object of God's affection. At Mount Sinai, He took on the role of the suitor, asking for her hand in marriage. He was to be their God; they were to be His people.

Jewish literature describes the giving of the Torah at Mount Sinai as a betrothal and a wedding. In Jewish wedding custom, the wedding vows are written out in a formal legal document called a *ketubah*. The contract spells out all the terms and conditions incumbent upon the bride and groom. It is a covenant document. Typically, the married couple displays the *ketubah* prominently in their home as a piece of artwork celebrating their union. Even in modern Western weddings, the repeating of vows retains vestiges of these nuptial contracts.

The rabbis compared the Torah to a *ketubah*.[16] Where God is likened unto the groom and Israel is likened unto the bride, the Torah is likened unto the *ketubah* that spells out the terms and conditions of their marriage. The Ten Commandments form the summary of their marital statement. Treasured like the *ketubah* in the married couple's home, Israel kept the tablets of the Ten Commandments inside the ark of the covenant at the center of the Sanctuary.

LEGALISM VS. OBEDIENCE

God did not give Israel the Torah as a means to attain salvation. The idea that one must, or even can, merit salvation merely through obedience to the commandments of the Torah is true legalism. The Torah paints a very different picture: one of salvation and redemption. When God gave Israel the Torah at Mount Sinai, they were already a redeemed people.

According to the Jewish numbering of the Ten Commandments, the first commandment is not the prohibition on idolatry; it is a simple acknowledgement that God exists. In Exodus 20:2, the LORD declares, "I am the LORD your God who brought you out of the land of Egypt, out of the house of slavery." In the days of the apostles, this simple statement was regarded as the first of the Ten Commandments.

Redemption must precede commandments. The salvation of Israel from Egypt physically dramatizes our own salvation from sin and death. In the story of the exodus, we learn that before we can receive the Torah, we must already be "saved."

Israel did not earn salvation from Egypt on the basis of obedience to the commandments. The people were already redeemed (on no merit of their own) before they received the laws at Sinai. Thus, the first declaration, "I am the LORD your God who brought you out of the land of Egypt," reminded the people that God had already redeemed them. Only because they were already saved were they able to receive God's commands.

True legalism continually attempts to reverse this process by claiming that one's obedience to certain commandments (or all the commandments) is the mechanism by which salvation is earned and a prerequisite to eternal life. The first of the Ten Commandments directly contradicts this notion. Salvation and relationship with God precede the Torah.

I have met many Christians who avoid learning the Torah because they are afraid of falling into legalism. But obedience is not legalism. If keeping the Torah were necessary for salvation, we would all fail because "all have sinned and fall short of the glory of God" (Romans 3:23). The Torah was never meant to be the means by which a person could earn his salvation. Legalism says, "I must obey God in order to be saved." Grace says, "I must obey because I am saved."

So what is the Torah? The Law, a target, the aim, the instruction of God, God's teaching, God's revelation, the five books of Moses, the whole of Scripture, a covenant, both the old covenant and the new covenant, a *ketubah* ... There must be a shorter explanation. Actually, the Torah can be summed up in just a few words. In the next chapter, we will read a story from Jewish literature about summing up the Torah.

CHAPTER FOUR

Summing Up the Torah

When Yeshua was a little boy and not yet known to the world, a certain Gentile who had lost faith in idols decided he would rather worship the God of Israel. He had one problem. The problem was what the Jews called their Torah: the Law.

THE MAN WHO STOOD ON ONE FOOT

"I want to know this God now," the man complained, "I don't have time to learn the whole Law." He thought about it for a while and came up with a plan. "I will go to the greatest sages and Torah teachers and have them teach me a short version of the Law."

In those days, the two most famous teachers of the Torah were the great sage Hillel and his colleague Shammai. Shammai was known for being a strict teacher. Hillel was known for being somewhat gentler.

The Gentile went first to Shammai. Shammai had a long measuring stick called a builder's cubit in his hand. The Gentile said to him, "Teach me the whole Torah, but do it while I stand on one foot."

Standing on one foot is easy to do for a short while, but after a few moments, you start to lose your balance. What the Gentile meant was, "Teach me the whole Torah, but do it quickly. No longer than just a minute or two!" He proceeded to stand on one foot.

Shammai could not believe his ears (or his eyes for that matter). "Who does this Gentile think he is? Teach the whole Torah while he stands on one foot? The whole Torah of Moses?" Shammai took his builder's cubit, whacked the tottering Gentile, and drove him away.

The Gentile thought, "I will try again." He went to Hillel and said, "Teach me the whole Torah while I stand on one foot."

Without hesitation, Hillel said, "What is hateful to you, do not do to your neighbor. That is the whole Torah. The rest is the commentary on it. Now go and study the rest."

The Gentile was still standing on one foot, but Hillel was done. The Gentile went away and began to study.[17]

THE BUILDER'S CUBIT

Let's take a look at some of the deeper meanings of this story. Why was Shammai holding a builder's cubit? Perhaps he was a carpenter. If so, he would not have been the only first-century rabbi to make his living in carpentry. Perhaps the measuring stick is meant to represent the Torah. The Torah can be compared to a builder's cubit.

The cubit was the basic unit of measure in the biblical world. A cubit is the length from the elbow to the tip of the finger. But as ancient carpenters must have discovered, using one's arm as a ruler has an obvious drawback—the measurement will be subjective, depending entirely on the arm-length of who is doing the measuring. The average man's arm length will approximate a cubit, but that will hardly be exact enough for building something. Imagine two carpenters framing the same building. One has short arms; the other has long arms. Each one builds his side of the structure twelve cubits high. What will happen? The building will be lopsided.

This can be compared to subjective morality. God has given us all an innate sense of right and wrong. A conscience. But it is subjective. What is right or wrong for me might not seem right or wrong for you.

To solve the cubit problem, the ancient world introduced the builder's cubit rod. It was a standardized unit of measure. If a board needed to be twelve cubits long, the carpenter could measure that length exactly. He could be confident that your cubit was the same as everyone else's.

The Torah is like the builder's cubit rod. To speak figuratively, it could be compared to the length from God's elbow to the tip of His finger. It is His standard, an objective standard of right and wrong.

It is not based on what feels right for me or does not feel right for me. It is black and white; it is right and wrong; it is thou shalt and thou shalt not; it is clean and unclean; it is holy and profane. It is a universal standard of righteousness. That's how Shammai used it. He used the builder's cubit to beat up the man. He used it to drive him away. He summed up the Torah by giving the man a sound bruising while he stood on one foot.

Whenever we compare ourselves to God's righteous standard, we will experience the same bruising.

DO UNTO OTHERS

When the Gentile came to Hillel and said, "Teach me the whole Law while I stand on one foot," the rabbi replied, "That which is hateful to you do not do unto others. The rest is commentary; now go and study."

Did Hillel mean that the other commandments were irrelevant? Did he mean that nothing else in God's Word mattered other than being civil and avoiding injury? Of course not. He was a teacher of the Law. He was not issuing a new law or an improved Word of God. Rather, he distilled God's Word down to its essence.

One generation later, Yeshua told His disciples, "So whatever you wish that others would do to you, do also to them, for this is the Law and the Prophets" (Matthew 7:12). Did Yeshua mean that the other commandments were irrelevant? Did He mean that nothing else mattered? Of course not. He also told them, "Whoever then annuls one of the least of these commandments, and teaches others to do the same, shall be called least in the kingdom of heaven; but whoever keeps and teaches them, he shall be called great in the kingdom of heaven" (Matthew 5:19).

A generation later the famous Rabbi Akiva declared that the commandment to love one's neighbor as oneself is the greatest principle in the Torah. Jesus Himself placed the commandment "Love your neighbor as yourself" second only to "Love the LORD your God with all your heart, and with all your soul, and with all your mind and with all your strength" (Mark 12:30–31).

Do you see a pattern developing? Hillel, Yeshua, and Akiva all taught that the result of Torah, the guiding principle of Torah, the heart and center of Torah, and every true extension of Torah is love.

Let's check with one more rabbi on the topic. After the days of Yeshua, but before the days of Akiva, a rabbi named Paul wrote on this topic. In Romans 13, while addressing Gentile believers in Yeshua living in Rome, Paul said:

> Owe nothing to anyone except to love one another; for he who loves his neighbor has fulfilled the law. For this, "You shall not commit adultery, you shall not murder, you shall not steal, you shall not covet," and if there is any other commandment, it is summed up in this saying, "You shall love your neighbor as yourself." Love does no wrong to a neighbor; therefore love is the fulfillment of the Torah. (Romans 13:8–10)

Paul succinctly stated this premise in Galatians by saying, "For the whole Torah is fulfilled in one word, in the statement, 'You shall love your neighbor as yourself'" (Galatians 5:14). But wouldn't it be absurd to take that as a blanket justification for disregarding whatever commandments we don't like on the basis that as long as we love one another, nothing else matters? One might just as effectively suggest, "As long as I love my neighbor, it is all right to eat whatever I want, do whatever I want, and sleep with whomever I want." But that would not be demonstrating real love, would it?

So what is real love? The Torah defines love with commandments that instruct us how to treat one another. All the commandments in the Torah that involve our obligation to our brother or our obligation to our neighbor are commandments about love. The commandments are acts of real love. Love is not the replacement of the Torah; it is the summary of the Torah. Or, as Akiva put it: It is the greatest principle of the Torah.

Love God and love your neighbor. Yeshua said, "On these two commandments hang all the Law and the Prophets" (Matthew 22:40 NKJV). We can compare the Torah and the Prophets to a jacket and trousers hanging on a clothes hanger. One does not discard the jacket and trousers and dress himself in the hanger! Rather, the hanger holds the jacket and trousers together. Love of

God and love of neighbor holds the Torah and the Prophets, with all their commandments, together.

That is why the practice of God's Word must result in love. For example, if I set out to keep a particular commandment but find myself arguing, insulting, and embittering others over it, then I may have kept the commandment, but I have failed to keep the Torah, because the Torah's essence is love. Love of God and love of neighbor.

In the Romans 13 passage, Paul stated that the commandments could be summed up in loving one's neighbor. Therefore, breaking the commandments is the opposite of love. The opposite of love is not hatred; it is selfishness. Love of self.

The commandments teach us to love others as ourselves. Submitting to the commandments displays God's love because those commandments are contrary to our lazy, selfish nature. When we truly keep the commandments about how to treat one another, we are truly loving others. And when we truly love God and others, we will keep the commandments.

LOVE MADE COMPLETE

How ironic that we might take the words of Paul and Yeshua, who tell us the commandments are summarized in love, and use those words as a justification for breaking the commandments. "I don't need the letter of the law because I am under the law of love." When Paul indicated that the entire Torah could be summed up in a single command, he joined his voice to the voice of Yeshua and to the voices of the most famous rabbis of Judaism. Love is a summary of the commandments, and the commandments are all acts of love:

> The one who says, "I have come to know Him," and does not keep His commandments, is a liar, and the truth is not in him; but whoever keeps His word, in him the love of God has truly been perfected. (1 John 2:4–5)

We must protect the biblical concept of love from being so generalized that it loses all meaning. Love is to be the preeminent virtue practiced by believers. Love summarizes the Torah, not by rendering all other requirements inconsequential, but by its very nature as the foundation of the Torah's requirements.

The New Testament was not advocating a 1960s hippy ideal where love becomes its own law without definition or boundary. The idea that the Christian heart defines its own standards based on the vague ethos of love is a delusion.

THE WOMAN CAUGHT IN ADULTERY

Some people think of the Torah as a harsh and cruel standard of law that needed to be mitigated by the gentleness and love of Jesus in the New Testament. For example, the famous story in John 8 tells of a time when the scribes and the Pharisees brought a woman caught in adultery before Yeshua. At the end of the story, Yeshua told the adulterous woman, "I do not condemn you" (John 8:11). He sent her away free of punishment—obviously a loving thing to do. But if the Torah really demands that a person caught committing adultery should be stoned (and it does), then Yeshua broke the Torah by letting her go, didn't He?

But wait! If Yeshua broke the Torah, then He sinned by letting her go. After all, sin is transgression of the Torah.[18] And if He sinned, then He cannot be the sinless Redeemer. This story needs a closer look.

THE NEW LAW OF LOVE?

Some teach that Yeshua set aside the old law of punishment and wrath in favor of a new law of love and mercy. Under the old law, the woman would have been stoned. Under the new law of love, she is absolved. But Yeshua told us that we must never think that He came to do away with the Torah of Moses. He doesn't allow that kind of thinking. Something else is going on in the story.

The gospel writer tells us the religious officials were using the question as a trap, in order to have a basis for accusing Yeshua. "Now in the Torah Moses commanded us to stone such women; what then do You say?" (John 8:5).

The clever trap works similar to the way the question about paying taxes to Caesar worked. No matter how He answered, they had grounds to form an accusation against Him. If Yeshua said,

"Stone her," they could accuse Him before the Romans because the Romans had recently taken the power of capital punishment away from the Sanhedrin.[19] The Jewish court no longer had legal authority to stone anyone. (Incidentally, that is why they needed Pilate to execute Yeshua, as it says in John 18:31, "We are not permitted to put anyone to death.")

On the other hand, if He said, "Show some love and let her go," they could accuse Him of advocating lawlessness. "This man teaches against the Torah of Moses," they could have claimed. "He sanctions adultery."

The ancient sages recognized that God's strict Word must be mitigated by God's love and mercy whenever possible. Just as God always had mercy on Israel, so too, love must be shown to others. After all, the Torah says "Love your neighbor as yourself" (Leviticus 19:18). For that reason, the sages of the Sanhedrin would normally try to avoid issuing a death sentence. One ancient Jewish source says, "A Sanhedrin which executed a person once in seven years was called murderous."[20] However, the judges of Israel were bound to keep the letter of the law. They could not arbitrarily set aside the Word of God on the basis that they felt compassion or pity for the accused. So what did they do? How did they show love while still keeping the law? Being good lawyers, they used legal loopholes.

LEGAL LOOPHOLES

In most cases, they employed the legal loophole of disqualifying the witnesses. The Torah says that every allegation must be established by two eyewitnesses.[21] If a crime had no valid eyewitnesses, then the case had to be dropped, even if the person's guilt was otherwise obvious. Oftentimes, judges disqualified the witnesses before the trial even began "unless the person was known to lead a reputable life and be utterly disinterested."[22] A relative of the accused, an enemy of the accused, or anyone with a shady reputation was automatically disqualified. Their testimony could not be considered reliable.

Without reliable eyewitnesses, God's Word did not allow a trial or punishment to take place.

Even if the case went to court, the judges attempted to disqualify the testimony of the witnesses through vigorous cross-examination. In a popular legend similar to the story in John 8, the Prophet Daniel presided over a trial where a woman was falsely accused of adultery.[23] Through cross-examination, he disqualified the witnesses and the woman went free.

Yeshua employed a similar approach. Rather than try to defend the woman (who really was guilty) or bend the law (which does not bend), He disqualified the witnesses. He did it through what appears to be supernatural means. He said, "He who is without sin among you, let him be the first to throw a stone at her" (John 8:7). According to the Torah, only qualified eyewitnesses could cast the first stones. Each man present was supernaturally conscience-stricken. "When they heard it, they began to go out one by one, beginning with the older ones, and He was left alone, and the woman, where she was, in the center of the court" (John 8:9).

Without witnesses, there is no trial. Without witnesses, the Torah says that the woman must go free. Yeshua asked her, "Woman, where are they? Did no one condemn you?" (John 8:10).

Through a legal technicality, He freed her from the punishment of the Torah. The important thing to realize, however, is that He did so within the boundaries of the Torah. Like the sages and Torah-lawyers of His day, He was able to avert the death penalty by disqualifying the witnesses. Unlike the lawyers of His day, Yeshua did it without investigation or cross-examination. He let each man's own heart and conscience condemn him.

Contrary to the opinion that this story shows how Yeshua disregarded the Torah in favor of a new order of love and grace, the story actually shows how He used the Torah's commandments to save the woman. The Torah says there must be two witnesses. By the time Yeshua was done writing in the dust, no witnesses remained to lodge an accusation. The Torah saved the woman.

By disqualifying the witnesses and releasing the woman, Yeshua escaped the religious leaders' clever trap. At the same time, He felt genuine compassion for the woman. As He sent her away, He told her, "I do not condemn you, either. Go. From now on sin no more" (John 8:11). He used the Torah to save her, then placed the Torah of His love before her as a pathway to turn her life to the Father. "From now on sin no more."

Yeshua Himself is not above the Torah of God, for it is His own law. Yeshua is God's Word made flesh; how then could He teach against God's Word? If He could have dismissed the Torah's requirement with a wave of his hand, there would have been no need for Him to suffer and die. God could have chosen to have arbitrary mercy upon us.

Instead, in order to save us, He employed another technical loophole in the Torah. By taking on the full measure of the Torah's punishment, Yeshua used the Torah, and the rules of the Torah, to save us. By satisfying the demands of the Torah with His own righteous life and innocent death, He set us free from condemnation. Like the woman in the story, He sets us free from condemnation and then, like the woman in the story, tells us, "I do not condemn you, either. Go. From now on sin no more."

That is the Law of Love.

WHILE STANDING ON ONE FOOT

When the Gentile came to Shammai and said, "Teach me the whole Torah while I stand on one foot," the sage replied by smacking him with the builder's cubit. The builder's cubit symbolizes the Torah and its commandments: God's standard of righteousness. The Torah provides a standard by which we must measure ourselves. But if the Torah can be compared to the span from God's elbow to the tip of His finger (as it were), we should also understand that God's arm is the measure of Torah, and God's arm is the arm of love. The Torah measures in love. Hence the wisdom of Hillel's answer. The outcome of Torah—the ultimate result—is a measure of love.

We all fall short of the Torah's standard of righteousness. The builder's cubit smacks all of us, but the outcome is love, as it says:

> For God so loved the world, that He gave His only begotten Son, that whoever believes in Him shall not perish, but have eternal life. For God did not send the Son into the world to judge the world, but that the world might be saved through Him. (John 3:16–17)

The love that brought the incarnation, the crucifixion, and the resurrection is the same love that gave the Torah. The exodus from Egypt, the voice at Sinai, the Ten Commandments, the books of Moses, and the covenants with Abraham, Isaac, and Jacob—all of these were acts of love.

Now, let's go and study.

CHAPTER FIVE

Torah and the New Testament

> And He came to Nazareth, where He had been brought up; and as was His custom, He entered the synagogue on the Sabbath, and stood up to read. (Luke 4:16)

Sometime near the outset of His ministry, Yeshua returned to His hometown, the village of Nazareth. On the Sabbath, He attended the synagogue. Luke points out that this was His custom, which is to say, He never missed Sabbath services.

YESHUA READS THE TORAH

We do not know exactly how first-century Galileans conducted a Sabbath synagogue service. Luke chapter 4 provides the oldest existing description of any synagogue service, and the details there are sparse. Nevertheless, most of the conventions one might find in any modern Sabbath synagogue service seem to have been present. Luke describes a public reading from the Torah, a reading from the Prophets, and a related teaching. Things have not changed much since then.

Luke tells us He "stood up to read." Anyone unfamiliar with the synagogue might understand that phrase to be merely an introduction to the following statement that He read from the scroll of Isaiah. That is, to say, He stood up to read from the scroll of the Prophet Isaiah. From a Jewish perspective, however, the words "He stood up to read" indicate that He stood to read from the Torah scroll. In the synagogue service, the reader called up to read from the Prophets must first read the last few verses of that week's Torah portion. That Yeshua went on to read from the scroll of the Prophet Isaiah indicates that He was the last reader called to read the Torah that Sabbath.

If the synagogue service in Nazareth bore any resemblance to later modes of Jewish worship, we have a good idea of what it probably looked like. A synagogue official opened the ark in which the scrolls were kept and removed the scroll of the Torah from inside it. In a solemn procession, he placed it on the platform from which it would be read. The synagogue attendant opened the scroll to the appropriate reading for the day and called a series of seven readers to take turns reading through the day's passage.[24] The first reader he called was a priest; that is, someone descended from Moses' brother Aaron. The second reader was a Levite. Any Jew in the community could be called up for the remaining five readings.

As the guest of honor that Sabbath, Yeshua was not called to read until the seven readers had stood to read before Him. The place of the eighth reader was a special honor because the eighth reader also read from the Prophets.

After the seventh reader had sat down, the synagogue official called out across the congregation, "Approach, Yeshua. Arise, Yeshua ben Yosef." Luke tells us He then "stood up to read" (Luke 4:16).

After Yeshua finished reading the appropriate portion from the scroll of the Torah, the official rolled the Torah scroll and set it aside before handing Him the scroll of Isaiah. Yeshua opened the scroll and found the place from which He would read.

He completed the reading, rolled the scroll of Isaiah back up, and sat down. This does not mean that He returned to His seat in the congregation but that He sat down to teach. In those days, Jewish teachers sat to deliver their discourses. When Luke says that He "sat down" (Luke 4:20), he employs the ancient equivalent of saying that He stepped up to the pulpit. Everyone's eyes were riveted on Him because He was to deliver the teaching that day—and He did. He taught from the Old Testament. After all, the Old Testament was the Bible Jesus read.

THE BIBLE JESUS READ

In his book *The Bible Jesus Read*, best-selling author Phillip Yancey observes that Yeshua did not have a New Testament in His Bible. The New Testament had not yet been written. But neither did His Bible have an Old Testament. No one thought of God's eternal Word as an 'Old Testament.' In the days of Yeshua, the Old Testament was simply called the Scriptures.

Today, some Bibles are printed without the Old Testament. They begin at the Gospel of Matthew. Even when our Bibles do contain the Old Testament Scriptures, they are not always read. Those books are typically regarded as a long introduction to Matthew. Though Christians study it in Sunday school and enjoy reading select stories, few regard the Old Testament as relevant for how to live the Christian life.

How sad to think that today's followers of Yeshua today rarely read the Bible He read. We have surprisingly little interest in the Scriptures that shaped His life and teaching. We regard the Bible of Yeshua as irrelevant. But is it really?

Yeshua didn't think so. He said that those Scriptures testified about Him.[25] He quoted them in order to correct and rebuke people. He interpreted them to give His disciples guidance. He quoted verses from Deuteronomy to defeat the devil in head-to-head spiritual warfare. His first recorded words after His baptism are quotations from the Torah of Moses[26] and His last utterance from the cross was a quotation from the Psalms of David.[27]

Yeshua spent the day of His resurrection discussing those old Scriptures with His disciples. He showed them the things written about Him "in the Torah of Moses and the Prophets and the Psalms."[28] There is certainly a lot of "Old Testament" in the New Testament.

The Bible itself refers to neither the Hebrew Scriptures (the ones we call "old") nor the Apostolic Scriptures (the ones we call "new") as old or new. These traditional appellations are actually counterproductive to seeing the Scriptures as God intended us to see them. If anything, we should be amazed at how the Hebrew Scriptures and the Apostolic Scriptures seamlessly connect into one continuous revelation.

Paul once wrote to his student Timothy, saying, "All Scripture is inspired by God and profitable for teaching, for reproof, for correction, for training in righteousness; so that the man of God may be adequate, equipped for every good work" (2 Timothy 3:16–17). But Timothy did not have a New Testament; his Bible was the Hebrew Scriptures. Could Paul really have expected believers to be taught, rebuked, corrected, trained, and equipped for good works from the Old Testament?

Yeshua and Paul and all the 'New Testament' writers regarded the Hebrew Scriptures—particularly the five books of Moses—as the bedrock on which they built their teaching. To them, those books were the only Scriptures. Paul did not know that his epistles would one day be collected as Scripture. He did not imagine himself writing new books of the Bible. He did not even live long enough to see the written Gospels produced. As far as Paul knew, the Hebrew Scriptures were the only Scriptures.

How odd for us to imagine that those Scriptures are not relevant to believers today. They were certainly relevant to Yeshua and Paul. They didn't just use them for teaching, rebuking, correcting, and training in righteousness; they lived their lives by them. Near the end of his life Paul declared himself fully obedient to the Torah of Moses.[29] Yeshua, of course, never broke a commandment of the Torah.[30] As followers of Yeshua and students of Paul, perhaps we should emulate their attitude toward the Old Testament.

In fact, we should probably consider using the term "Hebrew Scriptures" to describe the Old Testament. While they certainly are old, they contain the eternal, living words of God. Containing scrolls first committed to writing some 3,400 years ago, the Hebrew Scriptures are truly ancient; but they are by no means obsolete. They are "living oracles."[31] They reveal the person of Messiah.[32] They contain the glory of the new covenant.[33] They are the standard of righteousness for which we are to train. They equip us to perform the good deeds we are called to do.[34] They comprise the Bible Jesus read.

THE PARTS OF THE BIBLE

A foolish man set out to build a house. He wondered where to begin. "Should I build the front door first?" he wondered. "Perhaps I should start with the kitchen, or maybe the master bedroom. Better yet, I should build the roof first so I don't get rained on while I'm working."

Everyone knows that to build a solid structure, a builder must start with a foundation. After the foundation is laid, the first floor of the house can be built upon it. The second floor can be added to the first. The roof, which rests over the structure, is built last. Common sense, right? Yet for some reason, we often fail to apply such simple common sense to the interpretation of Scripture. We tend to want to start by building the second floor and the roof.

Just as a house is comprised of different parts, the Bible contains different types of books. The Hebrew Scriptures contain the Torah, the Prophets, and the Writings.

As we have already learned, the Torah consists of the five books of Moses. The Prophets include the oracles of the Prophets and the books of Samuel and Kings. The Writings include works of poetry (like Psalms and Song of Songs), wisdom literature (like Job and Proverbs), and short narratives (like Ruth and Ezra).

Judaism uses the acronym *Tanach* to refer to the Old Testament. *Tanach* stands for "Torah (*Torah*), Prophets (*Nevi'im*), and Writings (*Ketuvim*). Yeshua Himself referenced this threefold division of the Scriptures.[35]

Similarly, the Apostolic Writings (New Testament) are comprised of several parts. They include the Gospels, the Epistles, and the Apocalypse of John. All the Scriptures work together to form the whole structure, but they each have a different function.

THE SCRIPTURES	
Hebrew Scriptures (OT)	***Apostolic Scriptures (NT)***
Torah	Gospels and Acts
Prophets	The Epistles
Writings	The Revelation

BACKWARD AND UPSIDE DOWN

If your church experience has been at all like mine, you've spent most of your Bible study time reading and teaching from the Pauline epistles. We also study the Gospels and Revelation. Beyond those, we sometimes dabble in the Psalms and Writings, occasionally consult the Prophets, and once in a while glance at the Torah. Our priority of Scripture has the Epistles first and the Torah last. We read Scripture backward because we have been led to believe that Paul (the writer of most of the Epistles) taught against Torah, and Yeshua (in the Gospels) did away with Torah. Therefore we regard the Torah and Old Testament as less relevant and authoritative than our New Testament books. But this is backward and upside down. It is like building the second floor of the house before laying a foundation or building the first floor. We have the priority of Scripture wrong.

The correct priority of Scripture is sequential. We should start at the beginning. Paul teaches that a later covenant cannot contradict an earlier covenant.[36] Neither can a later Scripture contradict an earlier one. If there were such a contradiction, it would indicate that one of the Scriptures was wrong (in which case it cannot be inerrant Scripture) or that God had changed His mind (in which case He must be inconsistent and fallible). Since the Scripture is not wrong and God does not change, the correct priority of Scripture starts with the Torah.

THE PRIORITY OF SCRIPTURE

The Torah can be likened to the foundation of a house because, like a foundation, the Torah came first. It was the initial revelation of God. When God spoke the Torah through Moses, He introduced Himself to Israel and the entire world. Through the books of Moses, God made His debut to humanity. The Torah introduces us to who God is, what He is like, how He made the world, why He chose His people, how He redeemed them, and what He expects from them. It records God's covenants with His people, and it contains the stipulations of those covenants. Therefore, the Torah comes first. Any subsequent revelations, prophecies, or Scriptures need to be checked against the Torah for authentication. Any prophet who utters a prophecy contrary to the Torah is a false prophet.[37] A false prophet's writings cannot be regarded as Scripture.

The writings of the prophets are built upon the foundation of Torah. They presuppose the authority of the Torah and continually point back toward it. The consistent message of Israel's prophets called the nation to repent and turn back to the covenant norms expressed in the Torah. "Repent because you have broken the Torah," the prophets said.[38] The prophets also looked forward to the kingdom of heaven on earth—a time when God's Torah will be universally obeyed.[39]

The Writings are also built upon the foundation of Torah. Books like Proverbs continually exhort the reader to turn to the Torah.[40] The Psalms praise God's Torah and urge the reader to keep His laws.[41] Ezra tells the story of how a great national revival turned the nation back to the Torah. Any Israelite book that in some way contradicted the Torah would not have been regarded as Scripture. Consistency with the Torah was the primary litmus test of scriptural authenticity.

The New Testament stands on the same foundation. The Gospels record that Yeshua proclaimed a message of repentance.[42] He called His people back to the simple truth of Torah and offered His life as a payment for transgressions against the Torah.[43] To validate His teaching He continually quoted the Hebrew Scriptures.[44] He forbade His disciples from imagining that He might do away with the Torah and even encouraged them to keep the smallest of commandments.[45]

The Epistles extended and amplified Yeshua's teaching, but they rested on the foundation of Torah. The Epistles rarely quoted Yeshua to prove a point or to introduce a new teaching; instead the apostles cited passages from the Hebrew Scriptures and from the Torah. Paul continually spoke of the Torah, citing passage after passage from the Torah and the Hebrew Scriptures to make his case for the gospel. He found his source of authority in the Torah.

Even the Apocalypse of John stands on the foundation of Torah. It contains seemingly endless allusions to the Torah and speaks of the triumphant overcomers as those "who keep the commandments of God and hold to the testimony of Yeshua."[46] The Torah contains God's commandments. The testimony of Yeshua is the gospel. Those who overcome are those who keep the Torah and hold to the gospel. In this way, the book of Revelation alludes to the whole of Scripture while calling its readers to keep the commandments of God and the testimony of Yeshua. It's like the roof covering the entire structure.

FIRST THINGS FIRST

Yeshua quoted and cited the Torah to make His arguments and prove His identity. Paul also quoted and cited the Torah to make his arguments and prove Yeshua's identity. It would be illogical, then, to suppose that Yeshua and Paul, in the next breath, denied the Torah's authority. According to God's own criteria, any prophet who contradicts His Torah is a false prophet.[47] Therefore, if we encounter a passage in the Apostolic Scriptures that appears to contradict an earlier revelation of Scripture, then we are misunderstanding the passage. This is not to say that one Scripture is more important than another. It does not mean that Torah is more important than the Gospels or the Epistles. But it does mean that Torah must be regarded first, because it was given first. The latter writings presuppose our familiarity with the Torah and must therefore be interpreted in light of it.

The Prophets, Writings, Gospels, and Epistles all base their authority on the Torah of Moses. If we pull the Torah out from under them, they all collapse, and we are left with a hopeless jumble of confusing Scriptures that seem to contradict one another.

This explains why many believers find the Bible so hard to understand. It can be compared to beginning a novel in the last chapter. You would not know who the characters are. You would not know the setting or the plot. You would be left trying to piece together the storyline and making all sorts of assumptions that the author never intended. It makes much more sense to start at the beginning of the book.

In the same way, when we start in the Gospels and Epistles, we are learning about Messiah, but we haven't a notion of what a messiah is or what He is about. We are assuming a knowledge of the God of Israel, but we don't know anything about Him or Israel. We are engaged in conversations about laws we never learned. We are talking about sin and forgiveness, but we don't even have a standard definition of what a sin is. All Scripture is God-breathed and equally true and relevant, but let's get first things first.[48] Only when we start with the beginning of the book will we fully understand the middle and the ending. Only after we first lay the foundation of a house can we proceed to build the rest of the structure. When the house rests on a solid foundation, it is unshakable.

The bedrock on which the Bible stands is the revelation at Mount Sinai.

CHAPTER SIX

The Giving of the Torah

At Sinai God came down onto the mountain. That moment marked a permanent change in faith and religion. No longer was it valid to say, "Whatever you believe is true for you." Or, "Well, I think God is like this," or "My god isn't like that," or "My god is such-and-such." At Mount Sinai, theology ceased to be speculation and became the study of revelation. At Mount Sinai, God told us who He is; that telling is the Torah. The Torah is His message to us human beings, His self-disclosure, through Moses and the people of Israel.

Before the giving of the Torah at Mount Sinai, we human beings had no way of knowing who God was, what He was like, what He was about, or what He wanted. We had no way of abstracting or comprehending His blessed eternal self. How could we have known the unknowable? We could not have, and we did not.

So we imagined God within our own minds. We saw the sun and imagined a sun god. We saw the moon and imagined a moon god. Theology was speculation at best and superstition at worst.

You might object and say, "Surely Adam and Eve and Noah and the patriarchs and all those godly men in the book of Genesis knew God before the giving of the Torah at Mount Sinai." That's fair. But how is it that we know the stories of Adam and Eve and Noah and the Patriarchs? We know about them because their stories appear in the Torah. The book of Genesis can be regarded as divine revelation only because of what happened in Exodus 19–20. If not for the giving of the Torah in Exodus 19–20, we would not possess the knowledge of God that the patriarchs possessed.

The Mount Sinai epiphany was not given to one individual. A whole nation heard God speaking. Many people heard the words coming forth from the mountain. Most of the world's major religions trace their faith back to the spiritual endowment of a single individual. Premises of theology, faith, and creed are often built upon the subjective experiences of a single person. Not so with Torah. God gave the Torah to an entire nation. All the people of Israel heard the voice and saw the fire. It was God's big entrance.

He said, "*Anochi Adonai Eloheicha.*" "I am the LORD your God."[49]

It was an amazing, unparalleled debut onto the scene of human history. It was as if God said, "Hi, I'm God. Allow me to introduce myself."

NATURAL LAW

Why did God reveal Himself to humanity? Was it simply revelation for the sake of revelation? Was it simply an introduction? "Hi, I'm God. How are you? By the way, I made this place." Perhaps God saw it as a chance to impress us with thunder and lightning. No, God's revelation at Sinai was deliberate. He came down onto the mountain for a reason. He gave the Torah for a purpose. He gave us His laws.

Not that we didn't have any laws prior to Mount Sinai. We had laws. Every human society has laws.

Every society conducts itself under some code of behavior. The code may be explicit like the legal codes of Hammurabi, or it may be implicit, like the unwritten laws of hospitality that govern the East. But without a common code of conduct, a society could not be a society. Though ethics may vary dramatically from culture to culture, the existence of and need for some kind of ethical system is universally acknowledged. Notions of right and wrong and fair and unfair and honor and dishonor appear to be hardwired into human consciousness. Those primal notions emerge in every human association as some sort of code of behavior. We refer to this impulse toward ethical society as Natural Law.

Natural Law tells us that there is such a thing as wrong and right. It is the primal and universal conscience. Perhaps we learn it as children from parents and adults; perhaps we possess some innate moral compass, which, at a minimum, distinguishes between fair and unfair. Perhaps it is merely our capacity for empathy. Whatever the case may be, we can agree that every human society has some set of values.

We may differ on the specifics of exactly what is wrong and what is right, but as C.S. Lewis pointed out in his apologetics, we all seem to possess a notion that there are right things and wrong things.[50] From where does such a universal notion come? If we are just highly evolved animals, how can we account for this tendency toward moral categories?

The presence of Natural Law in human society is the result of being made in the image of God. We possess a moral conscience. Individually, and in association with one another, a pattern of morality emerges because God has made us moral creatures with an instinctual tendency toward distinguishing between right behavior and wrong behavior. We are intuitively aware of justice and injustice and the need for a system of rules to accommodate justice.

In Romans 2, Paul points out how the tendency toward Natural Law reflects God's law. He says:

> For when Gentiles who do not have the Torah do instinctively the things of the Torah, these, not having the Torah, are a law to themselves, in that they show the work of the Torah written in their hearts, their conscience bearing witness and their thoughts alternately accusing or else defending them. (Romans 2:14–15)

In this way, Paul says, we find within us a reflection of our Creator. Our natural desire for justice and fairness reveals a Maker with similar impulses.

CREATING GOD IN MAN'S IMAGE

By observing a work of art, one can deduce a thing or two about the artist who created it. By observing ourselves, we can deduce a thing or two about God.

Even before Mount Sinai, we were able to conclude that our Creator must have a moral drive similar to our own. If we have a conscience and feelings of right and wrong, this must be something that our Creator possesses.

But Natural Law as expressed in human beings and human societies is deficient. Sin corrupts us, and ever since Adam and that whole business with the serpent, we no longer accurately reflect the image of the Creator who made us. Even the best human efforts to live according to a moral code are flawed. The most moral of human societies are full of injustice and immorality. Human ethics are mutable. Moral absolutes without a higher authority are an impossibility.

While we may have an innate sense of justice, it is a slippery justice that we are willing to apply to others but rarely to ourselves.

From the early beginnings of human religions, the capriciousness of our own behavior had us imagining gods that were just as capricious as we are. We imagined gods motivated by human impulses of selfishness, lust, greed, and envy. We imagined the laws governing their behavior to reflect the uncertainty of our own human waywardness.

Our absolute moral authorities—i.e., the gods of the ancient world—were hardly in a position to issue moral imperatives. They were as sinful and petty as we are because they were, at best, merely projections of our own selves.

Short of direct revelation from heaven, how else were we to imagine God? If we had to base our assessment of God only on human behavior, God would come out looking human. We would have to surmise that the Creator possesses the same uncertain and twisted sense of subjective morality that we do, or He must be completely amoral, without connection or concern for human behavior. Both of these versions of God have been put forward at various points in human history. The classical gods of ancient Greece follow the former line of reasoning while Plato's monotheism ultimately arrives at the latter. It's not an attractive choice. On the one hand we might have gods who are as ill-tempered and unpredictable as we are, and on the other hand we might have a god who is completely dispassionate and uninterested in our affairs.

Fortunately, God did not leave us to speculate. At Mount Sinai, He gave us His laws.

REVELATION THROUGH LEGISLATION

If I were a god about to reveal myself to my creation for the first time, I would probably compose a friendly systematic theology to put into the hands of creatures so they could understand me and the universe I had created. I might throw in some convenient math equations to explain the recipe of my godhead. A few diagrams would be useful too.

God doesn't do things like I would.

When God revealed Himself to us, He did not give us a systematic theology, creeds, recipes, or diagrams. He gave us a legal code. He gave us laws.

They are more than just laws intended to tidy up human society. They are actual pieces of godliness. Each *mitzvah* (commandment) conveys a small revelation of God. More than just a rule for governing human behavior, the laws of Torah reflect the Lawgiver.

Yeshua told us that "the mouth speaks out of that which fills the heart" (Matthew 12:34). When God broke the silence and spoke to His creation at Mount Sinai, the words He spoke were the fullness of His heart. Each law, each commandment, no matter how small or seemingly irrelevant, descended as a piece of revelation from God, an overflowing of His heart.

For example, one of the laws given at Mount Sinai talks about enemies and donkeys. Exodus 23:5 says, "If you see the donkey of one who hates you lying helplessly under its load, you shall refrain from leaving it to him; you shall surely release it with him."

The law commanding us to assist our enemy when he is in difficulty reveals to us a piece of true godliness. It is a revelation of God that would never have occurred to us naturally. Such a law teaches us about God's mercy and compassion.

Even a moral human being would not feel compelled to help an enemy stand his donkey back up. Your enemy is the person who wants to hurt you and your family. Most of us would rejoice at the sight of our enemy's overturned donkey! We might offer a few encouraging hand gestures, but we certainly would not offer any assistance. Such a commandment is beyond the demands of Natural Law and far beyond the scope of human mercy and compassion. It betrays an origin other than human beings. It is a piece of God.

Comprehending the infinite God is beyond the scope of finite human beings. We could never begin to fathom even a single attribute of God. For example, we do not possess the faculties to wrap our minds around the depth, width, and breadth of God's mercy and compassion. We don't have the capacity to understand even that single piece of godliness. However, we all have enemies, and we have all seen donkeys. Enemies and donkeys are two tangible realities that we can easily comprehend. The Torah conveys to us a piece of godliness through a medium we can understand. When we study the law of helping your enemy stand his donkey back up onto its feet, we have learned a little bit of God's character.

ABOLISHING GOD

Because Torah is both law and revelation, it functions in a dual capacity. On the one hand, it provides a rule of conduct by which we are held accountable. On the other hand, it expresses God in human terms. Torah is more than just legal formulations; it reveals the person of God dressed in laws and commandments. The Torah is God's spoken word written down—His self-disclosure to the world.

When one realizes that God discloses Himself to the world in the Torah, one must also recognize the enormous gravity of declaring parts of that same Torah null or void. Even the smallest commandment of the Torah comes to us suffused with godliness. To declare any commandment as irrelevant or obsolete denies the eternal and unchanging nature of God.

As soon as we begin to discard commandments, we have begun editing God. We have started reshaping God into an image we deem more appropriate.

For example, we Westerners find the idea of Levitical purity laws (the laws of clean and unclean) disquieting. It is theologically convenient for us to annul all laws pertaining to Levitical purity. By so doing, we are able to clean up God's image a bit. We feel more comfortable with a God who doesn't make seemingly superstitious distinctions between a woman who is menstruating and one who is not. But in so doing, we have changed God's self-disclosure to suit our biases. This makes for a slippery kind of religion.

When we try to change the Torah or do away with a commandment, it is God we are trying to change or do away with.

WRITTEN ON OUR HEARTS

The Torah functions as both law and revelation. As such, when we live our lives according to its commandments (as they pertain to us), we are living out a revelation of godliness. Outside observers should be able to look at the Torah-observant life and discern godliness. Deuteronomy 4:5–8 says that when Israel lives out the Torah, the world will see God.

Needless to say, nobody's perfect. Neither Israel nor any other group of people has ever lived out God's standards perfectly. Even when the people of Israel have been righteous and God-fearing on the whole, the hearts of men and women are still errant and disobedient. There is a big difference between God's law, our notions of Natural Law, and our behavior. We rarely live up to our standards, much less to God's. The Torah is the substance of which our deficient Natural Law is only a shadow. A great divorce remains between God's law and human beings.

This explains why Messiah is necessary. In Messiah, the perfect revelation of godliness is fully realized. Living in complete accordance with God's law, Messiah offers a tangible and intimately knowable representation of the unknowable God. He is the Torah lived out.

The Messiah reconciles the human race to God's Torah. The ultimate completion of His work will occur when the Natural Law of human society is identical to the revealed law of Torah. A day is coming when the Torah will be written on the hearts of men and women in vivid detail. Jeremiah 31:33 says, "I will put My Torah within them and on their heart I will write it." This is the promise of the new covenant.

What does it mean to have the Torah written on our hearts? How is that different from the universal principle of Natural Law? When God's Torah is written on our hearts, there will be no disparity between the Natural Law of humanity and God's revealed Torah. Instead of vague and subjective notions of wrong and right, the Torah of God will be the natural impulse of human morality. In that day, human beings will accurately reflect God, fulfilling our destiny to be the image of God on earth.

Often, however, we labor under the false impression that this prophecy has already been completely fulfilled in us. Because we are part of the new covenant (to which Jeremiah was referring) and because we have received the Holy Spirit of God within us, we assume that we must already have God's perfect law placed in our minds and written on our hearts. But is God's Torah really fully written on our hearts?

Many theologians assume that it is. Believers sometimes foolishly suppose that since God's law is written on their hearts, they should allow their hearts to dictate their behavior. The reasoning goes something like this: "It doesn't feel like dietary standards are written on my heart. Therefore, these laws have been done away with and I need not follow them." But where do we stop with that kind of thinking? One might just as well say, "Since covetousness is written on my heart, the law that says 'Do not covet' has been done away with." Such a theology elevates our feelings and inclinations to become the arbiters of truth.

Jeremiah's prophecy of God's Torah being written on the hearts and minds of men and women has not yet been fully realized. Redemption is a process. The Torah is being written on our hearts, but none of us have arrived yet. For this reason, we are still in need of Yeshua. He remains the only man to have ever lived life as a perfect expression of God. He remains the only man with the Torah written in full upon His heart. Consequently, we are still very much in need of the written Torah. It remains the only standard we have to measure our errant hearts against.

LITTLE MOUNT SINAI

Writing the Torah on the hearts of the redeemed is the Holy Spirit's job.[51] Paul encourages us to rely more and more upon that inner Torah of God's Spirit. He reminds his readers in Galatia that the acts of the sinful nature are obvious, but against the fruit of the Spirit there is no Torah.[52] The Holy Spirit of God is at work within us as a new Natural Law, and as long as we are in obedience to the Spirit, we are not breaking Torah.

The Spirit will never lead us to break Torah. On the contrary, the Spirit of God is writing Torah onto the hearts of men. As we follow Yeshua and listen to the Spirit of God within us, we are being transformed into living Torahs, living revelations of godliness.

We are like little individual Mount Sinais.

God introduced Himself to the world at Mount Sinai. Through the giving of laws and commandments, He revealed His essential person to humankind. But that revelation is not a static one-time event. God's people must live out those laws and continue to reveal Him to the world. We are to be a perpetual Mount Sinai experience to all of creation. In that endeavor, we have had varying degrees of success and failure, but Messiah has truly accomplished the life of perfect obedience. Now, via the work of His redemption and the transforming power of His indwelling Spirit, God is conforming us to the image of Yeshua. He writes a living copy of the Torah on our hearts. This inner Torah does not negate the written Torah. Instead God's law will become a moral reflex for us, a new Natural Law, which will enable us to walk in genuine obedience. To the extent that we do so, we will be living lives like Messiah, perfect revelations of godliness in human form. This is what it means to be transformed by Messiah.

We can sum it up quite simply. When you see the donkey of someone who hates you fallen down under its load, and you immediately recognize that the right and moral thing to do is to help him stand his donkey back up, and you do it, then you are on the path to godliness.

CHAPTER SEVEN

The Inner Torah

In the story of Snow White, the wicked queen asks her magic mirror, "Mirror, mirror on the wall, who's the fairest of them all?" The mirror answers, "Snow White is fairest of them all." That was not the answer she wanted.

Many of us have had similarly bad experiences with mirrors. When we ask our bathroom mirrors, "Who is the fairest of them all?" the mirror shows us someone else. It is as if the mirror says, "I don't know who is the fairest, but it sure isn't you." Oh well; looks aren't everything. After all, beauty is only skin deep. A person might have other qualities hidden beneath the surface, right?

THE SOUL MIRROR

But what if you had a very different kind of mirror—a spiritual mirror that reflected your inner self? You could call it a "soul mirror." Imagine looking into your bathroom mirror, and instead of seeing your familiar face, you saw a brutally honest reflection of your soul and all the secret inner things of your heart. Suddenly on display were all the little sins, secret thoughts, pettiness, and lusts that are tucked away deep inside. How horrible it would be to find yourself confronted with your own soul, scarred and disfigured by a life of sin. Beauty really is only skin deep. What's under the skin is less than beautiful.

If you had such a mirror, would you want to look into it? Probably not. But James the brother of Yeshua tells us that we do have such a mirror. It is the Torah:

> Prove yourselves doers of the word, and not merely hearers who delude themselves. For if anyone is a hearer of the word and not a doer, he is like a man who looks at his natural face in a mirror; for once he has looked at himself and gone away, he has immediately forgotten what kind of person he was. But one who looks intently at the perfect law, the law of liberty, and abides by it, not having become a forgetful hearer but an effectual doer, this man will be blessed in what he does. (James 1:22–25)

James calls the Torah the "perfect Torah," and the "Torah of liberty." I have never looked into a mirror and thought of my reflection as perfect or liberating. Something else is at work here with this marvelous mirror.

The Torah is a soul mirror. What we see when we look into it is not a reflection of who we are on the outside, but a reflection of who we are on the inside. When a believer looks into the soul mirror of Torah, the reflection he sees staring back at him is not that horrid sin-scarred visage he might expect. He does not see his own image at all. He sees the reflection of Yeshua. That's how the Torah's soul mirror works. Disciples of Yeshua find their true identity in Messiah.

Seeing Yeshua in the mirror reminds us that we need to be conformed to this inner identity. We need to be obedient to the commands of God as the Master, Yeshua, was. Regardless of our own sins and failings, our true identity is the perfect and liberating reflection of Messiah. Therefore, the Torah mirror is the perfect Torah and the liberating Torah because it reflects Messiah within us—the one who perfects and liberates.

THE REFLECTION OF MESSIAH

When we turn away from that soul mirror, we risk forgetting the image we saw in the reflection. James says that the person who reads the Torah but does not do what it says is like that person who sees his reflection but then forgets what he looks like.

When we look into the Torah, we look into the righteousness of God. It shows us things with which we must deal, commandments to keep, dangers to avoid, and areas in our lives that need to be set right. What we do with that information is up to us.

Our goal should be to remember the face in the mirror. We need to carry that image into our daily lives. Somehow, we must overcome our forgetfulness. We should consciously choose to remember the image in the mirror. It is, after all, who we really are.

For believers, the Torah is not a sterile list of rules. It is a written version of our inner identity: the Messiah. We follow it because it is written on our hearts. It defines who we are as new creations.

James urges us to stare intently at our reflection in the Torah, and then to go out and practice what we have learned. The man who looks into the Torah but does not do what he learns there is like the man who forgets what he looks like. By obeying the commandments that apply to us, we express our inner identity on the outside. James essentially says, "Look in the mirror, and do something about what you see. Wash your face, comb your hair, and brush your teeth. Don't just walk away like a man who forgets what he looks like."

THE KIND OF PEOPLE WE ARE

To the extent that we live out the commands of Torah as they apply to us as Jews or as Gentiles, we are living out the righteousness of Messiah.

For example, take the commandment to immediately pay the poor man his wages. The Torah says that we must not make needy people wait for their earnings. Instead, we are to compensate them for their work that same day:

> You shall not oppress a hired servant who is poor and needy, whether he is one of your countrymen or one of your aliens who is in your land in your towns. You shall give him his wages on his day before the sun sets, for he is poor and sets his heart on it; so that he will not cry against you to the LORD and it become sin in you. (Deuteronomy 24:14–15)

When we look into the soul mirror of Torah and come across this commandment, we see the reflection of a generous and considerate person who is quick to help those less fortunate. The face in the mirror is the face of a man (or woman) who does not take advantage of the needy, but goes the extra distance, even inconveniencing himself, to make sure others' daily needs are met. It is the face of a fair employer who treats his employees with dignity and concern. He considers their personal estate before he considers the larger and more pressing concerns of the business.

If, after studying this principle, we return to our lives without implementing the commandment, we are like the man who forgets what he saw in the mirror. If we decide to withhold paying the contractor promptly, or to withhold paying a promised bonus until a more lucrative season, we have forgotten who we really are.

If, after studying this commandment, we eagerly apply ourselves to treating our employees and dependents with prompt consideration, then we are like the man who remembers what he saw in the mirror. We pay the contractor even before the thirty-day deadline because that's the kind of people we are. We pay out the promised bonus because our employees are anticipating it, even though it might make for a financial squeeze.

Consider the commandments of caring for the orphan, widow, and stranger; honoring father and mother; showing respect to teachers and elders; not coveting; not stealing; and not lying. Consider the implications of more obscure commands; the Torah commands one to drive away the mother bird before taking the young, and prohibits muzzling an ox while it treads out the grain. These are not stern and martial lists of "thou shalts" and "thou shalt nots." They are a reflection of our new identity. The Torah provides them to us as snapshots of who we really are in Messiah.

If we hope to enter into the full expression of our new identity in Messiah, we must be doers of God's Word, not just hearers. The Master tells us that a person who hears His words but does not do them is like a man who builds his house on the sand.[53] He is a man without foundation. James tells us that such a man is one who has forgotten what he really looks like. The Torah helps to keep us from forgetting; it shows us what we are supposed to look like.

NEW CREATION THEOLOGY

When we become believers, we become completely new people. The Bible tells us that we die to our old selves and are raised up as brand new human beings. Even though we are the same people on the outside, a new identity has been imparted to us. This identity is legal in nature. After becoming believers, we are legally adopted into God's family. We become sons of God. We are declared righteous—we are justified. Our sins are forgiven. Records of our guilt are erased. There is no condemnation. These are the legal aspects of our new identity in Messiah:

> Or do you not know that all of us who have been baptized into Messiah Yeshua have been baptized into His death? Therefore we have been buried with Him through baptism into death, so that as Messiah was raised from the dead through the glory of the Father, so we too might walk in newness of life. (Romans 6:3–4)

There are also aspects of this new identity that are more mystical than legal. Disciples of Yeshua receive a portion of God's Holy Spirit. He dwells within us. We actually become temples of the Holy Spirit. The Holy Spirit that dwells within us is the same Spirit that dwelt within and anointed Yeshua. Therefore, we say it is the Spirit of Yeshua that dwells within us. Indeed, "Messiah in you is the hope of glory" (Colossians 1:27). Messiah is being formed within you. Messiah dwells "in your hearts through faith" (Ephesians 3:17). "Do you not recognize this about yourselves, that Yeshua Messiah is in you?" (2 Corinthians 13:5).

Our new creation identity is premised on the notion that the Messiah now dwells within us, is being formed within us, and lives through us. This raises an important implication. There is a Torah-observant, Jewish person dwelling within you!

To the extent that we surrender our lives to this new inner identity, we succeed in living out our lives in Messiah. When we show the love of Yeshua to others, it is not our love we are manifesting, but the Master's love made manifest through us. Because Messiah dwells within us, acts of love we might bestow on others are actually His acts of love. We become, as it were, the hands and feet of Messiah. Our new nature—our Messianic nature—is revealed.

The same is true for every act of righteousness that we perform. Our good works are credited to Messiah. He lives through us.

When we continue in our old ways, walking in sin and lawlessness, we live in contradiction to our new nature. Sin conceals the Messianic identity within us. It obscures it.

When we keep the Torah as it applies to us as Jews or Gentiles, we allow Messiah to live through us. He is righteousness, and the Torah is the standard of righteousness. He is the law fulfilled, and He desires to fulfill it through us.

THE TORAH MADE FLESH

In the first chapter of his gospel, the Apostle John tells us that Messiah is the incarnate Word of God—He is the "Word made flesh." Through this divine Word, all things have been made. These words convey deep philosophical, theological, and mystical implications, but on the simplest level, it seems that the Apostle John alludes to the Torah. To him, the Word of God is first and foremost the Torah. He invokes the whole of the Torah with the words "In the beginning was the Word ...", and he returns to Torah in John 1:17 with his parallel statement: "For the Torah was given through Moses; grace and truth were realized through Yeshua Messiah."

The Torah is the Word that God spoke. All things are made through God's Word because He spoke His Word as recorded in the Torah, and all things came into being. The Torah is the will and wisdom of God; it is His self-disclosure to the world. As such, it is the extension of His being. In Jewish literature from around the first century, Torah is described as the Wisdom and the Word of God:

> I am the Word which was spoken by the Most High; it was I who covered the earth like a mist ... All this is the covenant book of God Most High, the Torah which Moses enacted. (Sirach 24:3, 23)

The theology in the Gospel of John had a short distance to go from a formulation like the one above where God is seen to be working in concert with the Torah, creating the world through the auspices of the Torah, to the expression we find in John 1:2. We need only remember that the Torah of God is His Word. Rabbinic literature makes that identification explicit on a number of occasions.

This does not at all mean that the Divine Word that was with God from the beginning is the actual written Torah as Moses knew it or even as we know it. Rather, the distinct essence of God—projected into the void and by which creation was created, ordered, and intersected—is the same essence that revealed the words of Torah to Moses and inhabited the body of Messiah. The self-revelation of God that resulted in the Torah of Moses at Sinai is the same self-revelation of God that created the universe. He is the light that shines in the darkness. He is the Torah made flesh.

This interpretation is consistent with how the earliest believers understood Messiah. Clement of Alexandria, one of the early church fathers, quotes a passage he ascribes to Peter when he says, "And in the preaching of Peter you may find the Master is called 'Torah and Word.'"[54]

Yeshua is not the same as the written Torah of Moses, but He is of the same essence as the Torah. One might speak of the five books of the Torah of Moses as the "Written Torah" and Yeshua as the "Living Torah." He is the Living Torah in that He emanates from the same source as the written Torah; that is, God's divine Word. He is the Living Torah in that He lived His sinless life in perfect accordance with the Torah. His life answers to all that is in the written Torah.

When we become His disciples, this Living Torah takes up residence inside us. He is the definition of our new identity. It stands to reason then that He leads us to keep the written Torah. The written Torah and the Living Torah work hand in hand. They work in concert to reveal the Word of God through us. "For the Torah was given through Moses; grace and truth were realized through Yeshua Messiah" (John 1:17).

The promise of the new covenant is this: "I will put My Torah within them and on their heart I will write it; and I will be their God, and they shall be My people" (Jeremiah 31:33). The Living Torah writes the commandments of the written Torah onto our hearts. That is Messiah being formed in us.

FAIREST OF THEM ALL

The Torah is like a mirror that shows us the face of Messiah within us. When we look into the Torah, we see the Master. He is on every page of it. He is the fulfillment of it. The commandments indicate how He lived His life and how He desires to live through us. Our highest goal in life should be to allow the inner Messiah to work through our outer man.

James tells us that when we obey the instructions we find in the Bible, we will be blessed in all that we do. When we look into the mirror and ask, "Mirror, mirror on the wall, who's the fairest of them all?" the soul mirror will tell us, "The One within you, living through you, is the fairest of them all."

CHAPTER EIGHT

Torah for the Sons of Noah

It's easy to see how the Torah applies to Jewish people, but what does the Torah have to do with Gentiles? God gave the Torah to Israel as a part of the covenant He made with the Jewish people. That's why people sometimes think that the Torah is only for the Jewish people. But the Torah has laws for all human beings, and it tells the story of a covenant that God made with all of humanity: the story of Noah and the Ark.

After the great flood, the LORD offered humanity a second chance. He made a covenant with Noah and his children:

> Then God spoke to Noah and to his sons with him, saying, "Now behold, I Myself do establish My covenant with you, and with your descendants after you." (Genesis 9:8–9)

A covenant defines a relationship between two parties. Every covenant entails terms and conditions incumbent upon both parties. For His part, the LORD promised Noah that He would never again flood the earth with water. For their part, Noah and his sons had to commit to maintaining certain standards of ethical conduct.

Jewish tradition explains the terms of God's covenant with Noah as consisting of universal standards called the Noachide laws. The sages taught that these commandments of the Torah apply universally to all human beings.

If there is no universal standard of right and wrong, how could God have punished the Gentiles in the story of Noah? Why did He punish the people of Sodom and Gomorrah? Why did He drive out the Amorites and Canaanites in the days of Joshua? How could He judge the nations if God imposed no standard of righteousness by which to make judgment? As Paul says, "Sin is not imputed when there is no Torah" (Romans 5:13).

NOACHIDE LAWS: Seven universal standards of Torah that apply to all humanity.

The rabbis derived seven laws of Torah that apply to all human beings. A literal reading of Genesis 9:1–6 reveals only a few general principles. The LORD commands the sons of Noah (that is, human beings) to reproduce and fill the earth. He commands them not to murder and not to allow a murderer to live. He allows them to eat whatever they want so long as they do not "eat flesh with its life, that is, its blood" still in it (Genesis 9:4). Obviously Genesis 9:1–6 does not provide an exhaustive list of rules to govern human morality and ethical conduct. We could call these rules the Four Laws of Genesis 9:

1. Be fruitful and multiply.
2. Do not eat meat with life/blood still in it.
3. Do not murder.
4. Put murderers to death.

The rabbis read between the lines of Genesis 9 and made some logical inferences to derive a total of seven general laws that they believed to be incumbent on all of humanity. They assumed that monotheism was self-evident as God speaks to Noah, so they wrote in two laws pertaining to belief in God: prohibitions on idolatry and blasphemy. They drew that conclusion from Bible passages that condemn the nations for the sins of idolatry and blasphemy. The rabbis understood the commandment to "be fruitful and multiply" as the antithesis of the sexual immorality that had corrupted the earth during the days before the flood, so they added a prohibition on fornication. Since God punished the people of Sodom and Gomorrah and the people of Canaan for sexual immorality, the sages argued that the prohibition on sexual sins must apply universally.

The rabbis also noted that the sin of robbery was one of the moral deficiencies that brought the flood, so they added a prohibition on theft to the list. Finally, they saw that the requirement for man to spill the blood of a murderer could be misunderstood as an endorsement of vigilante-style justice, so they steered its interpretation toward a civil form of jurisprudence by mandating the establishment of courts of law. These seven laws are called the Noachide Laws, i.e., the Laws of Noah:

1. Do not worship idols or other gods.
2. Do not blaspheme God's name.
3. Do not murder.
4. Do not commit sexual immorality.
5. Do not steal.
6. Do not eat things while they are still alive (i.e., meat with blood).
7. Establish courts of justice.

To be sure, these seven laws can be derived from one place or another in the Bible, if not directly from Genesis 9. They form a sort of minimalist approach to ethical monotheism: believe in God, be a decent person, be kind to animals, and settle your disputes in court.

Some rabbis had opinions about additional laws that should be added to the list, but most agreed on these seven.[55]

Does this mean that the Torah has only seven laws for the Gentiles? No. The seven laws of Noah function more like general categories. They serve as seven broad categories of Torah that encompass numerous specific commandments mentioned elsewhere in the Torah.[56]

1. IDOLATRY

The prohibition on idolatry applies to all human beings, both Jews and Gentiles. It includes the prohibition on making or honoring any physical representation of the Almighty and the prohibition on worshiping, sacrificing, or praying to any god other than the LORD. It includes the prohibition on worshiping any created thing, whether heavenly bodies, angels, animals, natural phenomena, trees, or human beings. It prohibits the creation of any object for purposes of veneration and worship. The prohibition on idolatry forbids us from bowing to an idol or showing it any form of service or even acknowledging that an idolatrous religion is true. Even if the idol is not present, it is forbidden to honor it. For example, pouring out a libation to a god before a meal qualifies as idolatry, even when no idol is present. One should be careful to avoid even the appearance of honoring an idol. The prohibition on idolatry forbids persuading others to practice idolatry. According to Jewish tradition, it also includes the prohibitions on occult arts, spell-casting, charms, spirit-channeling, fortune-telling, communing with the dead, sorcery, divination, and other magical rituals. In summary, the Torah's numerous laws that deal with idolatry pertain also to Gentiles.

2. BLASPHEMY

The prohibition on blasphemy applies universally to all human beings. Blasphemy entails cursing God or railing derisively against Him. The sages deduced from the story of Job that the prohibition on blasphemy applies to Gentiles. Job was not Jewish. When Satan struck him with many afflictions, his wife said to him, "Do you still hold fast your integrity? Curse God and die!" He replied, "You speak as one of the foolish women speaks. Shall we indeed accept good from God and not accept adversity?" In all this Job did not sin with his lips (Job 2:9–10).

Therefore, Jewish tradition prescribes a blessing even on the occasion of hearing bad news. Even if (God forbid) one hears terrible news, he should say, "Blessed be the True Judge."

The prohibition on blasphemy includes all the laws about sanctifying God's Name. For example, this law includes the prohibitions on making false oaths, swearing falsely in the name of the LORD, and taking the LORD's name in vain.

3. MURDER

The prohibition on murder applies universally to all human beings. After the flood, the LORD required Noah and his sons to henceforth pay for human life with the life of the murderer:

> Whoever sheds man's blood, by man his blood shall be shed, for in the image of God He made man. (Genesis 9:6)

God had allowed Cain to live, but after the flood, He required a murderer to be put to death for his crime. The new, rigid requirement prevented the rise of the same kind of unchecked violence that led to the flood in the first place.

Judaism distinguishes between murder and manslaughter. For example, killing in war, in self-defense, or as a punishment decreed by a court is not the same as murder.

In Jewish law, the prohibition includes the murder of the unborn and euthanasia.[57] One who is able to prevent the death of another and does not do so transgresses the prohibition against murder. The law forbids participating in murder in any form. The law against murder also includes the prohibition on suicide. It includes all the Torah's laws of manslaughter and the laws of the cities of refuge.

By extension, the laws against murder include the prohibitions on gossip, evil speech, and character assassination, which the Torah equates with murder: "You shall not go about as a slanderer among your people, and you are not to *act against the life of your neighbor*" (Leviticus 19:16).[58]

4. FORNICATION

The prohibition on fornication (*zanah*) and sexual immorality applies universally to all human beings. Jewish law interprets the prohibition on fornication to forbid sexual relations with anyone other than one's spouse. The rabbis derived the principle from Genesis 2:24: "A man shall leave his father and his mother, and be joined to his wife; and they shall become one flesh." Rashi, the famous Jewish commentator on the Torah, explains, "The Holy Spirit says this to forbid the Sons of Noah from forbidden relationships."

The exact definition of forbidden relationships for Gentiles was unclear in the days of the apostles. The rabbis taught that all the Torah's laws of sexual immorality also applied to Gentiles, but the extent to which they applied was debated.[59] According to one early rabbinic explanation, the rules of sexual conduct are much more stringent for the Jewish people than they are for the sons of Noah. The *Tosefta* says, "In regard to these forbidden relationships, the Gentiles are judged in accordance with their own laws."[60] This opinion created a significant gray area when it came to defining sexual morality for Gentiles. As we will see in the next chapter, the apostles clarified the ambiguity for Gentile disciples of Yeshua by prohibiting all forms of sexual immorality and holding them to the same standards that the Torah applies to the Jewish people. Therefore, the general prohibition on sexual immorality forbids Gentiles from homosexuality, bestiality, pedophilia, incest, adultery, prostitution, and sexual contact with anyone or thing outside of wedlock.

5. THEFT

The prohibition on theft applies universally to all human beings. This prohibition doesn't just apply to theft of personal property; it also prohibits kidnapping, all forms of malfeasance, swindling, extortion, and dishonesty for the sake of taking advantage of another. It prohibits overcharging, using unjust weights and measures, moving boundary stones, encroachment on another's livelihood, and all forms of dishonest or abusive business transactions. The law against theft prohibits withholding the salary of a worker. By means of creative exegesis, it includes the prohibition on rape and seduction (which involve the theft of sexual gratification). According to the same interpretations, cannibalism also falls under the prohibition of theft. Some authorities include the prohibitions on assault under the prohibition of theft. Others include the prohibition on coveting. In summary, the prohibition on theft includes all the Torah's laws that prohibit taking advantage of someone else.

Apostolic-era writers summarized the first five Noachide laws in a manual of discipleship for new Gentile believers titled the *Didache*:

> Do not murder. Do not commit adultery. Do not practice pederasty. Do not commit sexual immorality. Do not steal. Do not practice magic. Do not use potions. Do not murder children through abortion nor kill them after they have been born. (*Didache* 2:2)

6. LIMB OF A LIVING ANIMAL

The prohibition on eating things while they are still alive applies universally to all human beings. The LORD commanded Noah: "Every moving thing that is alive shall be food for you; I give all to you, as I gave the green plant. Only you shall not eat flesh with its life, that is, its blood" (Genesis 9:3–4). On the surface, this law sounds like similar laws in the Torah that prohibit Jews from ingesting blood or eating the meat of unslaughtered animals.[61] One verse from Deuteronomy, however, makes that interpretation impossible:

> You shall not eat anything which dies of itself. You may give it to the alien who is in your town, so that he may eat it, or you may sell it to a foreigner, for you are a holy people to the LORD your God. (Deuteronomy 14:21)

If the Torah advocates giving the meat of an animal that died of itself to a Gentile, then the law in Genesis 9:3–4 cannot be understood as a universal prohibition on the meat of unslaughtered animals. To reconcile the seeming discrepancy, the sages interpreted Genesis 9:3–4 as a prohibition on eating the meat of a creature while it is still alive, "with its life, that is, its blood." For example, a person might decide to amputate an animal's limb and eat it in order to save the rest of the animal for a later time. This would be forbidden.

This law hints toward other laws in the Torah, such as laws about treating animals in a humane manner and further dietary laws about proper slaughter and clean and unclean meat.

7. COURTS OF JUSTICE

The commandment to establish courts of justice that will carry out justice and maintain civil order applies universally to all human beings. The commandment is inferred from the statement to Noah, "Whoever sheds man's blood, by man his blood shall be shed." This law can be broadly read as a principle for justice, similar to the Torah's laws of "eye for eye." It is saying the punishment should fit the crime: measure for measure. This law also implies the existence of a court of law that can condemn the guilty, exonerate the innocent, and mete out punishment. The

Torah's many laws of justice, legal procedure, litigation, tort law, fines, penalties, and rules are included in this category. Jewish interpretation, however, does not hold a Gentile court of law to the standards of a Torah court of law. For example, circumstantial evidence is not permitted in a Torah court of law, but it is permitted in a Gentile court. Likewise, the testimony of only one witness might be allowed in a Gentile court. The rabbis made these allowances in order to validate the secular legal systems, but the allowances do not reflect the Torah's ideal. Ideally, a Gentile court of law would employ the same standards as a Jewish Torah court of law.

MORE THAN SONS OF NOAH

If Judaism already had in place a minimum standard of Torah to govern Gentiles, why did some Jewish believers insist, "It is necessary to circumcise them and to direct them to observe the [whole] Torah of Moses" (Acts 15:5)? Why did the apostles feel the need to issue the apostolic decree of Acts 15, listing four laws that apply to Gentile disciples? In the next chapter, we will read about the big argument in the book of Acts and find out why the Gentile disciples are more than merely sons of Noah.

CHAPTER NINE

An Argument about the Torah

In the days of the New Testament, a big argument over the Torah took place among the early disciples of Yeshua. Was it an argument about whether or not the new covenant canceled the Torah? Was it an argument about whether or not Jews should still keep the Law now that the Messiah had come, died for sins, and risen from the dead? No, not at all. No one thought the Torah was canceled, and no one suggested that Jewish believers in Yeshua no longer needed to observe the Torah's commandments. The argument was about something else altogether. The argument was about whether or not Gentile believers should be required to become Jewish and keep the whole Torah, just as the Jewish believers did.

THE ARGUMENT

Some apostles, such as Paul and Barnabas, believed that Gentiles did not need to become Jewish in order to become disciples of Yeshua and heirs of eternal life. They believed that the kingdom was big enough for all nations and that Gentiles should not try to become Jewish after becoming believers. In fact, this was Paul's one rule for all the churches:

> Was any man called when he was already circumcised? He is not to become uncircumcised. Has anyone been called in uncircumcision? He is not to be circumcised. (1 Corinthians 7:18)

It's important to know that the word "circumcised" is apostolic shorthand for "Jewish," and "uncircumcised" is apostolic shorthand for "Gentile." So Paul says, "I have one rule for all the churches. Was anyone Jewish when he became a believer in Yeshua? Stay that way. Was anyone not Jewish? Stay that way."[62]

CIRCUMCISED: Jewish

UNCIRCUMCISED: Gentile

Paul believed that Gentiles needed to keep the basic ethical standards of the Torah—essentially the equivalent of the seven Noachide laws—but they did not need to keep the commandments specifically given to the Jewish people as identity markers and tokens of the covenant, such as the sign of circumcision, the Sabbath and holy days, the complex dietary laws, various Levitical regulations, and ceremonial regulations. On the other hand, Paul taught that a Gentile who became Jewish was obligated to keep the whole Torah, just as the Jewish people are obligated. He said, "I testify again to every man who receives circumcision, that he is under obligation to keep the whole Torah" (Galatians 5:3).

That's how Paul saw it. He felt happy so long as the Gentile disciples consented to live by the basics of ethical monotheism, like the seven Noachide laws discussed in the previous chapter. But not everyone felt happy with that standard.

Some apostles taught that it was not sufficient for Gentile disciples to remain Gentiles. They taught that Gentiles did need to become Jewish in order to become disciples of Yeshua and heirs of eternal life. They told the Gentile disciples, "Unless you are circumcised according to the custom of Moses, you cannot be saved" (Acts 15:1). They claimed, "It is necessary to circumcise them and to direct them to observe the Law of Moses" (Acts 15:5). They reasoned that God had given the messianic promises to the people of Israel—the Jewish people. If Gentiles wanted a share in the kingdom of heaven, they needed to become Jewish.

DECISION IN JERUSALEM

The argument became so heated that the apostles decided to settle it in court. They took the question to a Torah court of law in Jerusalem presided over by the elders among the apostles. The judges included some of the Master Yeshua's original twelve disciples, such as Simon Peter, along with other notables, such as James the brother of the Master. Here's an overview of the trial:

THE ORIGINAL QUESTION

Must the Gentiles be circumcised (become Jewish) in order to be saved? (Acts 15:1)

> THE CHARGE: The Gentiles must be circumcised and required to obey the Torah of Moses. (Acts 15:5)
>
> THE REBUTTAL: Why do you put God to the test by placing upon the neck of the disciples a yoke which neither our fathers nor we have been able to bear? But we believe that we are saved through the grace of the Master Yeshua, in the same way as they also are. (Acts 15:10–11)
>
> THE PROOF TEXT: Amos 9:11–12 (David's Fallen Tabernacle) (Acts 15:16–18)
>
> THE DECISION: It is my judgment that we do not trouble those who are turning to God from among the Gentiles ... (Acts 15:19)

THE FOUR ESSENTIAL PROHIBITIONS:

But that we write to the Gentiles that they abstain

1. from things contaminated by idols
2. from fornication
3. from what is strangled
4. from blood. (Acts 15:19-20)

After much debate transpired, and "they were even more perplexed, Peter under the guidance of the Holy Spirit took the floor" and addressed the court.[63] He reminded the elders about the Cornelius incident in Caesarea, “Brethren, you know that in the early days God made a choice among you, that by my mouth the Gentiles would hear the word of the gospel and believe” (Acts 15:7).

Everyone remembered the debate sparked by that incident. They also remembered the signs and miracles associated with it: the appearance of an angel to a Roman centurion, how the angel revealed Simon Peter’s whereabouts in Joppa, Simon Peter’s vision of a sheet let down from heaven, the serendipitous arrival of the men from Cornelius, and the outpouring of the Spirit on Gentiles.

Simon Peter continued, “God, who knows the heart, testified to them giving them the Holy Spirit, just as He also did to us” (Acts 15:8). No one could doubt the authenticity of what had happened that day in Caesarea:

> The Holy Spirit fell upon all those who were listening to the message. All the circumcised believers who came with Peter were amazed, because the gift of the Holy Spirit had been poured out on the Gentiles also. For they were hearing them speaking with tongues and exalting God. (Acts 10:44–46)

Simon Peter interpreted this event as God’s own testimony on behalf of the Gentile believers. It indicated that He received them as they were, without any contingencies about future circumcision or conversion or Torah. Peter concluded, “Now, therefore, why are you putting God to the test by placing a yoke on the neck of the disciples that neither our fathers nor we have been able to bear?” (Acts 15:10).

The yoke is the Torah. The rabbis speak of the “yoke of the commandments” and the “yoke of Torah” as the authority of God’s Torah.[64] One who denies the existence of God and the authority of the Torah is said to “throw off the yoke.”[65] The Gentile proselyte who undergoes immersion to become Jewish accepts upon himself the yoke of the commandments at the time of his immersion.[66] One who neglects the Torah “lightens the yoke of Torah.”[67]

According to Simon Peter, requiring Gentile believers to undergo conversion (circumcision) and compelling them to keep the whole Torah of Moses is “putting God to the test” (which is just biblical language for “making God mad”).

GOD'S GENTILES

James the brother of the Master agreed. He found evidence in the biblical prophecies that the nations will play a big role in the kingdom. He pointed to a prophecy about the Messianic Era which declares that the restored Davidic kingdom will include Gentiles who bear God's name; that is, they belong to God:

> I will rebuild the Tabernacle of David which has fallen, and I will rebuilt its ruins, and I will restore it, so that the rest of mankind may seek the LORD, and all the Gentiles who are called by name. (Acts 15:16–17, quoting Amos 9:11–12)

The Gentile disciples of Yeshua fit the description of the prophecies: Gentiles from the nations who identified themselves with God's name and sought after God because of the revelation of the Davidic Messiah. If the apostles required those same Gentiles to become legally Jewish, however, they would cease to be "Gentiles who are called by God's Name." They would all be Jews. They would fail to fulfill the prophecy because a literal fulfillment of the prophecy requires that both Jews and Gentiles must exist in the Messianic Era.

THE DECISION

James declared, "It is my judgment that we do not trouble those who are turning to God from among the Gentiles" (Acts 15:19). That is to say, "We should not require the Gentile disciples to become Jewish and keep all the laws of the Torah that are incumbent upon us as Jews."

The decision exempted the Gentiles from circumcision and the particular commandments that pertain specifically to Jewish identity. It prohibited the Jewish believers from forcing those issues on Gentiles. Nevertheless, the apostles did not forbid the Gentiles from voluntarily participating in the Sabbath, the dietary laws, or any aspect of Torah-life.

THE FOUR ESSENTIALS

The Gentile believers did not need to become Jewish, but they did need to learn a few things about living among Jewish people. The LORD said, "If [the Gentiles] will really learn the ways of My people ... they will be built up in the midst of My people" (Jeremiah 12:16). To teach the Gentiles the "ways" of the Jewish people and establish them "in the midst" of the Jewish people, James recommended binding the Gentile believers with four prohibitions from the Torah. He said, "We should write to them to abstain from the things polluted by idols, and from sexual immorality, and from what has been strangled, and from blood" (Acts 15:20).

The four laws raise more questions than they answer. Why these four, and what do they mean? Are the four essentials a blanket exemption from the rest of Torah? Does it mean that if a Gentile just keeps these four laws, he can get away with breaking all the other laws in the Torah? Are these the only four prohibitions that apply to Gentiles? Why are three of them ceremonial and dietary while only one of them pertains to moral behavior? What, if any, relationship do these four essentials have with the so-called laws of Noah?

LAWS FOR STRANGERS WITHIN ISRAEL

If Judaism already had a minimum standard of Torah for Gentiles in place (such as the seven laws of Noah, which are explained in the previous chapter), why did the apostles feel it necessary to create this list of four specific prohibitions for Gentile believers? At first glance, it appears that some of the prohibitions are redundant. The apostles could have simply told the God-fearing Gentiles, "Keep the laws given to Noah."

The Gentile believers were more than "sons of Noah" or simple God-fearers. Through his allegiance to King Messiah, a Gentile believer entered into close fellowship with the Jewish people and became an adjunct member of the nation. In the language of the Torah, he became a *ger toshav*, i.e., "a stranger who sojourns among you."

GER TOSHAV: A resident alien, a stranger sojourning with Israel. A Gentile who lives among the Jewish people and therefore falls into a special category of the Torah's laws.

In the Torah, certain laws apply to both the Jew and the stranger who sojourns in the midst of the people of Israel. All four of the laws in the apostolic decree belong to that category of laws.

James rattled off a short list of commandments applying to Gentiles living in the midst of Israel. Each one goes beyond the universal laws of Noah. He seems to have derived them from Leviticus 17–18. In those chapters, the Torah describes the sins of the Canaanites, warns the people of Israel against imitating their ways, and prescribes four prohibitions that both the Israelite and the stranger who dwells within the nation must keep.[68]

The following short explanation of the four laws in the apostolic decree attempts to identify the source of each law in the Torah and briefly explain its implications for Gentile believers. (A fuller, more detailed discussion of each of the four laws appears in the appendix at the end of this book titled, "The Apostolic Decree.")

> Abstain from things sacrificed to idols and from blood and from things strangled and from fornication. (Acts 15:29)

1. "ABSTAIN FROM THINGS SACRIFICED TO IDOLS ..."

> They shall no longer sacrifice their sacrifices to the goat demons with which they play the harlot ... Any man from the house of Israel, or from the aliens who sojourn among them, who offers a burnt offering or sacrifice, and does not bring it to the doorway of the tent of meeting to offer it to the LORD, that man also shall be cut off from his people. (Leviticus 17:7–9)

The Torah prohibits making a sacrifice outside the Temple. This prohibition presupposes an idolatrous sacrifice. According to Leviticus 17, the stranger who dwells among the people of Israel is also prohibited from sacrificing outside the Temple, and by extension, from eating any type of food sacrificed outside the Temple.

This rule is not the same as a general ban on idolatry. Judaism includes the prohibition on idolatry in the universal laws of Noah that apply to all of humanity. The apostles did not need to restate that rule. Rather, the prohibition on "things sacrificed to idols" requires a heightened distancing from idolatry and from things polluted by idolatry.

2. "AND FROM BLOOD ..."

> And any man from the house of Israel, or from the aliens who sojourn among them, who eats any blood, I will set My face against that person who eats blood and will cut him off from among his people. For the life of the flesh is in the blood, and I have given it to you on the altar to make atonement for your souls; for it is the blood by reason of the life that makes atonement. (Leviticus 17:10–11)

The prohibition on blood is not, as some explain, a prohibition on murder. The apostles considered the law against murder as part of the universal laws of humanity given to Noah. They did not need to restate that rule because it had already applied to everyone since the days of Noah.

Nevertheless, the prohibition on blood still seems redundant since God gave a similar prohibition to Noah in Genesis 9:4. Why would the apostles repeat a prohibition that already applied to all Gentiles?

As explained in the previous chapter, Judaism interprets Genesis 9:4 to prohibit only the limb of a living animal. Therefore, according to the broad terms of ethical monotheism imposed by the synagogue, Gentiles were permitted to ingest an animal's blood so long as the animal is dead. This explains why the apostles needed to state the rule in no uncertain terms. The apostolic decree against blood clarifies that Gentile disciples fall into a different category. As strangers in the midst of the people of Israel, Leviticus 17:10–11 specifically prohibits Gentile believers from consuming any blood at all.

3. "AND FROM THINGS STRANGLED ..."

> Therefore I said to the sons of Israel, "No person among you may eat blood, nor may any alien who sojourns among you eat blood." So when any man from the sons of Israel, or from the aliens who sojourn among them, in hunting catches a beast or a bird which may be eaten, he shall pour out its blood and cover it with earth. (Leviticus 17:12–13)

The prohibition on "things strangled" refers to the meat of animals not properly slaughtered according to the ceremonial standards of Judaism. It includes all types of carcasses, and it includes animals that died of injury (other than ritual slaughter) or disease.[69] The Torah specifically allows non-Jews to eat a carcass, but it requires the "stranger who sojourns" within Israel to employ the Torah's method of slaughter, pouring out the blood upon the ground.[70] Since the Gentile believers fell into the latter category, the apostles forbade them from the meat of strangled animals. Essentially, this means that Gentile believers should avoid meat that has not been slaughtered and drained properly according to Jewish standards.

4. "AND FROM FORNICATION."

> But as for you, you are to keep My statutes and My judgments and shall not do any of these [sexual] abominations, neither the native, nor the alien who sojourns among you. (Leviticus 18:26)

The prohibition on fornication in Leviticus 18:26 comes at the end of a long list of forbidden unions (Leviticus 18:6–23). The list prohibits incest, intercourse with a woman in menstruation, adultery, homosexuality, bestiality and, by implication, all similar sexual deviancies.

The apostolic prohibition on sexual immorality might seem redundant since the seven universal laws of Noah already prohibited fornication. Why would the apostles repeat an obvious prohibition that already applied to all Gentiles? According to rabbinic explanation, the rules of sexual conduct are much more stringent for the Jewish people than they are for the sons of Noah. Jewish law said, "The Gentiles are judged in accordance with their own laws [of sexual morality]."[71] This opinion left the meaning of sexual immorality vague and undefined for Gentiles.

The God-fearing disciples, however, fell into a different category than the rest of the sons of Noah. As strangers in the midst of the people of Israel, the Torah holds them to the same standards of sexual purity to which it holds the Jewish people: "Immorality or any impurity or greed must not even be named among you, as is proper among saints" (Ephesians 5:3).

SOCIAL OBSTACLES

The apostolic decree requires believing Gentiles to abstain from meat contaminated by idolatry, from meats that are not slaughtered according to a kosher standard, from the consumption of blood, and from sexual immorality. The four laws are not a substitute for the rest of the Torah, nor are they meant as the four minimum commandments that will merit salvation. Since Gentile believers have been "grafted in" to the nation, the additional four laws apply to them, over and above whatever laws apply universally to all human beings.

The four laws also enabled Jews and Gentiles to congregate together more easily. Each law created an obstacle between the Gentile and social interaction with the idolatrous world. At the same time, the four laws removed obstacles to social interaction with the Jewish people.

The four laws ensured the Jewish community that Gentile disciples no longer participated in the local idolatrous shrines, meals tainted by idolatry, sexual promiscuity, and other pagan indecencies. The four laws brought Jewish and Gentile believers closer together in table fellowship by assuring the Jewish people that meat served by Gentile disciples was slaughtered in a kosher manner consistent with Jewish law.

MOST OF THE PROHIBITIONS

It's absolutely wrong to say that the Torah does not apply to Gentile believers. When we combine all of the seven Noachide laws and their various derivatives with the four laws of the apostolic decree and all of their implications, we discover that many of the Torah's 613 commandments, particularly the prohibitions, do apply directly to Gentile believers and are incumbent upon them. Therefore, one cannot say that the Torah is only incumbent upon the Jewish people. Most of the Torah's prohibitions apply equally to both Jews and Gentile Christians.

THE LAWS OF LOVE

Yet another category of the Torah's laws apply equally to Jews and Gentile believers. Jewish tradition states that the commandment to "love your neighbor as yourself" (Leviticus 19:18) refers only to one's fellow Jew. The Master Yeshua challenged this interpretation when He expanded the meaning of "neighbor" to extend to one's fellow human being.[72] Therefore, all the commandments that fall under the general category of "you shall love your neighbor as yourself" apply directly to Gentile disciples on the authority of the Master who said, "In everything, therefore, treat people the same way you want them to treat you, for this is the Torah and the Prophets" (Matthew 7:12). The apostles used that teaching as the basis for requiring the God-fearing Gentile believers to adhere to the Torah's commandments governing social interaction and human relationships:

> For the whole Torah is fulfilled in one word, in the statement, "You shall love your neighbor as yourself." (Galatians 5:14)

> He who loves his neighbor has fulfilled the Torah. For this, "You shall not commit adultery, you shall not murder, you shall not steal, you shall not covet," and if there is any other commandment, it is summed up in this saying, "You shall love your neighbor as yourself." Love does no wrong to a neighbor; therefore love is the fulfillment of the Torah. (Romans 13:8–10)

The "love your neighbor category" finds expression in the numerous apostolic references to "one another."[73] All the commandments in the Torah that relate to the way one should treat another, therefore, apply equally to both Jewish people and Gentile believers. Commandments pertaining to "your brother" and "your neighbor" and "one another" should be interpreted in like manner, i.e., incumbent upon both Jews and Gentile believers in their behavior toward both Jews and Gentile believers.

SABBATH, SYNAGOGUE, AND TORAH

> For Moses from ancient generations has in every city those who preach him, since he is read in the synagogues every Sabbath. (Acts 15:21)

James maintained that the God-fearing Gentile believers should be held to the legal standard that the Torah applies to a stranger in the midst of Israel even if they lived outside the geographical borders of the nation of Israel. He explained, "For Moses from ancient generations has in every city those who preach him, since he is read in the synagogues every Sabbath." Jewish communities and synagogues existed in almost every major population center in the Roman world and Mesopotamia.

In those days, the Gentile believers still assembled within those synagogues. They considered the synagogues (both messianic and non-messianic) as their houses of worship. Just as the Gentile believers had spiritually attached themselves to Israel, they literally moved among the people of Israel. Their presence in the Jewish communities of the Diaspora reinforced the need for adherence to the apostolic decrees. They were living as strangers among the Jewish people, just as the Torah indicated.

James could also depend on the Gentiles learning Torah—both the commandments that applied to them and those that were not incumbent upon them—as they attended the synagogue and heard the Torah read each Sabbath. Notice that James took Gentile participation in Sabbath and synagogue Sabbath services as a foregone conclusion. The apostles did not require the Gentile believers to observe the Sabbath, but they assumed that they would celebrate the LORD's holy day to some extent. They assumed that the Gentile believers would attend the prayer services and Scripture readings as they participated in Torah life along with the Jewish people, in accordance with the custom of the Master.[74] As yet, no alternate, competing holy days existed. The God-fearing Gentile believers participated in almost every aspect of Torah life—whether or not they were obligated to do so.

When considering the application of the apostolic decree in Acts 15, that broader context of Gentile believers participating in Torah, synagogue, and Jewish life must be kept in view. The apostles did not divorce the God-fearers from Judaism or Torah observance. They did not turn the Gentile believers away from the Sabbath, the festivals, or any of the other joys of Torah.

CHAPTER TEN

Torah Lost and Found

The Torah contains a law that says, "Anything lost by your countryman, which he has lost and you have found … you are not allowed to neglect … You shall restore it to him" (Deuteronomy 22:2–3). I have found something that you have lost, and I hope to restore it to you. The thing I have found is the Torah. It used to belong to you. Now I need to restore it to you. This is especially true if you are a Jewish disciple of Yeshua, but even Gentile disciples have a heritage in the Torah.

The writings of the New Testament are clear about this. The followers of Yeshua were Torah people. Yeshua Himself was a Torah teacher. He told His disciples to keep and teach the Torah, and He encouraged them to demonstrate their love for Him by being faithful to the commandments.[75] His Jewish disciples were once described as many myriads, "all zealous for the Torah" (Acts 21:20). But through the long years of waiting for His return, we have wandered far, forgotten much, and lost some things that once were of great value to us. We have lost the Torah and forgotten that it ever belonged to us.

ACTS 15 FOR JEWS

If you are a Jewish disciple of Yeshua, you may have noticed that the decision of the Jerusalem Council (which we explained in the previous chapter) was not about you. The question was about whether or not Gentile disciples needed to become Jewish and keep the whole Torah. It went without saying that, if they became Jewish, they would be obligated to keep the whole Torah as Jewish believers. Well—it almost went without saying. Paul actually did say it: "I testify again to every man who receives circumcision, that he is under obligation to keep the whole Torah" (Galatians 5:3).

Ironically, the question quickly reversed itself in Christianity. Until the recent advent of modern Messianic Judaism, Christian theology was universal in its position that a Jew could not become a disciple of Jesus unless he renounced Torah, Judaism, and Jewish identity. This is just the opposite of the same problem—a failure to distinguish between Jews and Gentile believers.

We misunderstood the intention of the New Testament, and we assumed that the decision in Acts 15 meant that no one should be Jewish or keep the Torah. That's why so many Jewish believers today are not Torah-observant. That's why so few Jewish believers practice Messianic Judaism today. Not only did we think that the decision of Acts 15 applied to Jewish believers, we also assumed that all Paul's letters to the Gentiles were also meant for Jewish believers.

Now, for the first time in centuries, we are beginning to understand the real intention behind Paul's epistles and the decision in Acts 15. The apostles agreed that Gentile believers did not need to undergo circumcision and full obligation to the Torah as Jews. *The obvious corollary requires that Jewish believers are obligated to observe the Torah.* The thought that a Jewish believer might also be exempt from the whole yoke of Torah did not enter the minds of the apostles.

Traditional interpretations assume that Acts 15 releases both Jews and Gentiles from keeping the Torah's ceremonial laws of circumcision, Sabbath, calendar, dietary laws, etc. On the contrary, the entire argument of the Jerusalem Council presupposes that those obligations remain incumbent on the Jewish believer.

We are not the first people to come to this realization. The nineteenth century Messianic Jewish pioneer, Rabbi Yechiel Tzvi Lichtenstein, discourses at length on this subject in his *Commentary on the New Testament.*[76] Lichtenstein was a devout, Torah-observant Jewish believer and a great Bible scholar who worked closely with Franz Delitzsch, translator of the Hebrew New Testament. Lichtenstein wrote commentary on the New Testament in Hebrew to accompany Delitzsch's Hebrew New Testament. The following section provides a translation from that Hebrew commentary on Acts 15.

THE JEWISH PEOPLE AND THE TORAH
YECHIEL TZVI LICHTENSTEIN

The apostles did not even consider that Jewish believers might be exempt from observing the Torah because they all knew the words of the Master: "I did not come to abolish the Torah," and that whoever abolishes one of the least commandments will be called "least." ... If he did not cancel the Torah, neither did his apostles have authority to abolish the Torah. Therefore, the apostles and the first believers among the people of Israel considered it absolutely foundational that a Jewish person must live according to the Torah since the Holy One, blessed be He, imposed it upon us. We are not free men entitled to desist from it. If we annul the Torah, we are guilty, for one who annuls the Torah is a sinner, and the Messiah was not made the servant of sin, as Paul said to the Galatians (2:17).

And we are forbidden to say, "If Messiah has already made us righteous to inherit eternal life, why do we still need to observe the Torah? Why should we obey it if it is not required for eternal life and we are saved only by faith?" We are forbidden to speak this way, for who are we to annul the Torah if the Messiah did not annul it? The Messiah was not made the servant of sin. This is similar to what some Christians say: "Why do I need to give charity to the poor or to do any other good deed? According to the New Testament, is not faith sufficient for me?" It is forbidden to speak like this, for he is a sinner who closes his fist, and the Messiah was not made the servant of sin. Therefore, faith does not benefit him, as it says in the Epistle of James 2:14, "What use is it, my brethren, if someone says he has faith but he has no works? Can that faith save him?"

John says, "Everyone who practices sin also practices lawlessness; and sin is lawlessness (1 John 3:4). Paul himself says in Romans 6:15, "What then? Shall we sin because we are not under law but under grace? May it never be!" And James says: "To one who knows the right thing to do and does not do it, to him it is sin" (4:17). It is a sin of omission. But when he repents and regrets the wickedness of his heart, then faith saves him by its power, as Paul also says in Acts 26:20: "Repent and turn to God, performing deeds appropriate to repentance." Then faith is beneficial.

And it is the same with the observance of the whole Torah for the Jewish people. We are compelled to observe it, even if the Torah feels burdensome to us. Neither does the Torah distinguish between commandments that are moral principles and those which are ceremonial and without explanation. The prophets made the ethical commandments the cornerstone, as did the teaching of the Messiah, but they did not annul the others. Yeshua said, "You have neglected the weightier provisions of the Torah: justice and mercy and faithfulness; but these are the things you should have done without neglecting the other commandments" (Matthew 23:23).

But since the Torah was weakened by the flesh (Romans 8:3), there is no one who does not sin and who fulfills the Torah completely. Therefore, we cannot attain eternal life through keeping the Torah or by our own effort (God forbid!). Only faith in the Messiah can accomplish that. Thus Paul wrote to the Romans, "Do we then nullify the Torah through faith? May it never be! On the contrary, we establish the Torah" (Romans 3:31). And faith came, "because by the works of the Torah no flesh will be justified in His sight ... for all have sinned and ... are justified as a gift by his grace through the redemption which is in the Messiah Yeshua" (Romans 3:20–24). This was foundational for all the believers and the apostles.

THE RABBIS ON ACTS 15

Rabbi Lichtenstein was a believer in Yeshua and a New Testament scholar, but he was not the only rabbi to study and explain the

New Testament. Rabbi Jacob Emden (1697–1776) was not a believer, but he saw both Yeshua and Christianity in a positive light. He pointed out that the apostolic decision in Acts 15 accords with rabbinic law, and he observed Yeshua and His Jewish disciples remained Torah observant:[77]

> The sages were the ones who forbade circumcising a Gentile who does not accept upon himself the yoke of all the commandments. Moreover, the sages said that the Gentile should not observe the Sabbath fully [as a Jew does]. The apostles of the Nazarene decided that, instead of circumcision, those Gentiles who do not enter the Jewish faith should practice immersion (after all, immersion is also a condition of full conversion), and they should practice a commemoration of the Sabbath ... But the Nazarene and his apostles were Jewish, so they observed the Sabbath and circumcision as mentioned earlier. They fully observed the Torah ... But even here [in Acts 15] they judged correctly as far as the Gentiles were concerned, for they were not commanded to observe it. Nor should one make it difficult for the Gentiles, since they were not the ones who accepted the Torah at Sinai and are not required to observe the 613 commandments. However, the matter is completely different for Jews, for Torah is incumbent upon them because God delivered them from the iron furnace of Egypt to be His possession. Therefore they and their children became subject to it forever. This, their covenant, will never be forgotten from their mouths, nor will it be abolished from their children. They have given their lives for it throughout the generations, as the Psalmist has recorded: "All this is come upon us, but have we not forgotten You, and we have not dealt falsely with Your covenant" (Psalm 44:18).

Rabbi Shimon ben Tzemach Duran (1361–1444) was not a believer either, but he read the New Testament himself and came to his own conclusions about the Nazarene and His first followers. He comments on Acts 15 as follows:[78]

> In all actuality, the intention of Yeshua's disciples was to lighten the yoke of the Torah and commandments from upon the Gentiles, in order to draw their hearts to the faith, because they saw that if they forced them to take up the yoke of circumcision and the yoke of practical commandments, they would not enter into their faith. But as far as Yeshua's intention for Jewish people, it did not even occur to him to change the Torah for them, nor for himself or for his disciples; after all, they were Jewish, and upheld the Torah themselves, as I have mentioned from their words. (Rashbatz, *Keshet Umagen*)

Even non-Messianic rabbis can read the New Testament and see the obvious implications of the ruling in Acts 15. The New Testament distinguishes between Jews and Gentiles. Not all of the commandments that apply to Jewish believers apply equally to Gentile believers. Not all of the exemptions enjoyed by Gentile believers should be enjoyed by Jewish believers.

GENTILE CHRISTIANS KEEPING THE TORAH

The decision in Acts 15 did not exempt Gentile disciples from all the Torah's commandments. If you are a Gentile Christian, you are probably already keeping most of the Torah as it applies to you. Just by living the Christian life, you are keeping most of the Torah. It is pretty obvious when you think it over. Consider the Ten Commandments, for example. Things like honoring one's father and mother, marital fidelity, and basic honesty are all commandments of Torah with universal application. The commands to care for the orphan and widow, look after the poor and extend a helping hand to a brother in need—those are all precepts of Torah that hang on the principle of loving your neighbor as yourself. Prohibitions on violence, injustice, theft, homicide, sexual deviancy, and occult practices are all examples of the basic moral statutes that comprise the laws of Torah and apply to all believers. Faith, grace, repentance, confession, prayer, and baptism are all found in the Torah as well. The things that define Christian life are Torah-based. For the most part, the Christian life is one of Torah lived out.

True, a lot of commandments are not part of the normal Gentile Christian's life. Take for example the numerous animal sacrifices of the Temple worship system. Christians don't bring sacrifices. But wait! Did you know that the Torah forbids everyone from sacrificing today? According to the books of Leviticus and Deuteronomy, sacrifices can only be made at the Temple in Jerusalem.[79] There has not been a Temple in Jerusalem since the days of the apostles. It would be a sin to offer animal sacrifices today because we have no Temple. The Bible says so. Therefore, every time we do not offer up burnt offerings in our backyard, we are keeping a commandment of the Torah: the commandment not to offer a sacrifice outside of the Temple in Jerusalem. Similarly, the strict measures of justice and punishment—stoning and the like—cannot be applied unless one lives in the land of Israel under the authority of a duly ordained Torah court of law like the Sanhedrin. Since there has not been a functional Sanhedrin wielding civil authority in almost two thousand years, there has not been a capital case tried in just as long. As much as we might sometimes like to throw stones at someone, the Torah forbids us from vigilante justice of that sort. Most of the laws of Torah that Gentile Christians do not keep are laws that do not apply under current circumstances. This is not to say that those laws are irrelevant or done away with, just that under current circumstances, they cannot be practiced.

Meanwhile, Christians are busily keeping the weighty matters of the Torah all over the world. Christianity has spread faith in the God of Abraham, Isaac, and Jacob to all nations. Christians everywhere are working to see justice done, to see the oppressed relieved, to see the hungry fed, and to see the kingdom of heaven advanced. Christians are famous for offering care and assistance to the stranger, orphan, and widow. The world may not want to admit it, but Christians are known for our high level of integrity, our moral character, and our scrupulous honesty. The church has some dark chapters in its history, and there are sometimes a few bad eggs in a basket, but generally speaking, Christians are respected, even if we are not appreciated. All these things are true because Christians, by and large, live out the Torah. Most Christians are Torah-observant without even knowing it because they are already keeping the laws of the Torah that apply to Gentile disciples.

Despite that, the Gentile church has lost its connection to the Torah. The apostles never intended to see the Gentile believers divorced from Judaism. Acts 15 was meant to keep Jews and Gentiles together, not to separate Gentiles into a new religion.

SOME THINGS WERE LOST

Even though the decision in Acts 15 exempted the Gentile disciples from observing certain ceremonial and ritual laws which are incumbent specifically upon the Jewish people, the Gentile disciples in the first century still looked more Torah-observant than most Messianic believers today. They worshiped in synagogues in the midst of the Jewish community. They had no days of worship or holidays other than those of the synagogue. They did not drive vehicles to get to their place of fellowship. In order to be able to share table-fellowship with Jewish believers in the community, they maintained the biblical dietary laws. They revered the Temple in Jerusalem and accompanied Jewish believers on pilgrimage to Jerusalem for the festivals. On one level or another, the New Testament-era Gentile believers engaged with the Torah's laws—even those that are no longer commonly practiced by Christians.

The church lost all of that surprisingly early in the development of Christianity. During the first and second centuries, the traumatic wars with Rome and the tumult of Roman persecutions deeply impacted the development of the young, emerging Christian church. In response to the Jewish uprisings, the Roman government under the Flavian emperors and again under Trajan and Hadrian unleashed punishing persecutions against Judaism. Heavy taxes combined with anti-Torah legislation, arrests, and persecutions made it unpopular to be identified with Torah or Judaism. At certain times, a person could be arrested for keeping the Sabbath or any other obvious Jewish practices. At the same time, Jewish leaders made a concentrated effort to push the Messianic believers out of the synagogue. Christianity lost her connection to Torah and the Jewish people. This happened in fulfillment of the Master's words.

Yeshua predicted the persecutions, and He predicted the coming time of lawlessness. He told His disciples:

> They will deliver you to tribulation, and will kill you, and you will be hated by all nations because of My name. At that time many will fall away and will betray one another and hate one another. Many false prophets will arise and will mislead many. Because lawlessness is increased, most people's love will grow cold. (Matthew 24:9–12)

The love of which He spoke was the love of God—the greatest commandment—and the love of neighbor. According to Deuteronomy 6:4–5, love for God is demonstrated by obedience to His commandments. Similarly, 1 John 5:3 states that "… the love of God [is] that we keep His commandments." When we turn away from the commandments, our love for God diminishes, and as our love for God diminishes, we turn further from the commandments.

Some early believers held on to Torah and their connection to Judaism. The writings of the church fathers and the writings of the rabbis attest to the existence of Torah-keeping Yeshua-followers well into the third century and beyond. Jewish believers especially maintained their connection to Torah observance, but most of the disciples of Yeshua left the old ways behind.

In the following chapters, we will look at a few of the things we inadvertently lost along the way. We will consider the biblical Sabbath, the biblical festivals, and the biblical dietary laws. If you are a Jewish disciple of Yeshua, I am delighted to have the opportunity to return these lost items to you, thereby fulfilling the verse that says, "You shall restore it to him" (Deuteronomy 22:2). If you are a Gentile disciple, I am delighted all the same because these things are part of your heritage as a believer, too. They are things we all lost a long time ago, and I am obligated to restore them to you.

CHAPTER ELEVEN

The Sabbath of the Torah

Every Friday night my family gathers around the table to welcome the holy day of rest. This has been our custom as long as any of my children can remember—since before some of them were born. Today they are young adults, but they still come home for Sabbath dinner on a Friday night.

THE BIBLICAL SABBATH

The house is full of good smells: hot soup, something in the oven, fresh bread. As dusk settles on the neighborhood the boys might be reading through the weekly Torah portion, preparing to contribute something at the Sabbath table. My wife or my daughter lights the Sabbath candles. Guests arrive at the door. My wife finishes the final preparations in the kitchen. She will not need to cook again for more than twenty-four hours. At the table, prayers are said, blessings are dispensed, songs are sung, and words of Torah are exchanged. The day of rest, the LORD's day, has begun.

I'm a Sabbatarian. That's a word that means someone who keeps the biblical, seventh-day Sabbath. Even though I'm not Jewish, I choose to keep the Sabbath as a day set apart for the LORD. That makes me a Sabbatarian. The members of my family are also Sabbatarians. So are the Jewish people.

SABBATARIAN: An observer of the biblical, seventh-day Sabbath.

God commands His people to cease from labor on the seventh day of the week. This day of rest is called the *Shabbat*. In English, we call it the Sabbath. Paul says that the Sabbath is a shadow of things to come and the substance of Messiah.[80] The Sabbath is about the Messiah. Therefore, the Sabbath has something for all the followers of Messiah—both Jews and Gentiles.

BLESSING AND HOLINESS

Out of all those things in this vast reality that we know as the creation, the Sabbath was the first thing that God set apart as holy. The Sabbath stands from the beginning of time as the first institution of godliness. Before there was a temple or an altar, before there was a Bible or a commandment, before there was a church or a single hymn was written, the Sabbath already existed.

Jewish people prize the Sabbath as a day of delight (*oneg Shabbat*). Messianic Jews guard and keep the Sabbath as a treasured and prized possession. It is the oldest heirloom they have inherited from the family of God. It is a sign of the covenant between God and Israel: "You shall surely observe My Sabbaths ... for this is a sign between Me and the sons of Israel forever" (Exodus 31:13,17). Observant Jews keep the Sabbath as a remembrance of the redemption from Egypt.[81]

Many Gentile believers, myself and my family included, also find delight in the Sabbath. These Gentile disciples keep it as a holy day to the LORD, a day of worship, a day for Bible study, and a day of rest. They keep the Sabbath along with the Jewish people as a sign of solidarity with the people of God and as servants of our Master Yeshua, as it says, "So that your male servant and your female servant may rest as well as you" (Deuteronomy 5:14). They keep the Sabbath as a remembrance of the six days of creation.[82]

As Jewish and Gentile followers of the Master, when we enter into the Sabbath, we encounter Yeshua in fresh, new, and delightful ways. The Sabbath is not burdensome, as some suppose. The Master of the Sabbath declares, "Come to Me, all who are weary and heavy-laden, and I will give you rest" (Matthew 11:28).

We receive the Sabbath as a gift, not as from a despotic ruler demanding our submission. The Sabbath gently beckons us, subtle and sublime, wrapped in garments of light, inviting us to meet with the LORD. We delight in the Sabbath because we encounter God within it.

THE SABBATH OF PEACE

The Sabbath is a day of peace. On the Sabbath, we set aside the cares of this world. On the Sabbath, we close the door to the troubles, stresses, and anxieties of this present age, and we enter into the calm spirit of peace that comes from the presence of Messiah. "Peace I leave with you; My peace I give to you; not as the world gives do I give to you. Do not let your heart be troubled, nor let it be fearful" (John 14:27), says the Master. On the Sabbath day, we quiet ourselves enough to feel the presence of His peace.

The apostles teach that the Sabbath foreshadows things to come.[83] The book of Revelation tells us that the coming of Messiah will institute a one thousand-year era of peace—the kingdom on earth, also called the Messianic Era. This one thousand-year era can be compared to the Sabbath. The six days of the week correspond to the six thousand years of redemptive history. "With the Lord one day is like a thousand years, and a thousand years like one day," Peter reminds us (2 Peter 3:8). The seventh-day Sabbath foreshadows the coming kingdom of heaven on earth—the Messianic Era.

These are not just Christian ideas. Even the rabbis of old believed that the Sabbath foreshadows the age of peace that Messiah will bring. The kingdom is called the day that will be entirely Sabbath.[84]

The prophets tell us that when Messiah comes, all mankind will keep the Sabbath. "'From sabbath to sabbath, all mankind will come to bow down before Me,' says the LORD" (Isaiah 66:23). Every time we keep the Sabbath, we receive a little foretaste of the perfect Sabbath rest and peace that will fill the world when Messiah comes.

THE SABBATH OF CREATION

When God rested on the seventh day, He ceased from His work. The Hebrew word for cessation is *shabbat*. The word Sabbath comes from *shabbat*. God did not rest from work on the seventh day because the six days of creating the universe had exhausted

Him. He ceased from work because He had finished the work. God rested from the work of creation. Therefore, on the Sabbath day, the Jewish people rest from the work of creating as well. Sabbath-keeping Jews cease from the work of shaping, creating, forming, making, ordering, structuring, organizing, mixing, and molding things to produce results. Imposing our will onto substance, and creating order from disorder, is the type of work prohibited on the Sabbath. Production is work. Creation is work. Making money is work. Sabbatarians cease from work as a remembrance of creation, and we cease from work to remember our salvation.

THE SABBATH OF SALVATION

As believers, we rest in Messiah. Hebrews 3–4 presents the Sabbath as a picture of the kingdom and the World to Come. The book of Hebrews compares salvation in Yeshua to the Sabbath. Those without faith in Yeshua, the writer of Hebrews explains, are like those without rest. He says, "There remains a Sabbath rest for the people of God. For the one who has entered His rest [the Sabbath] has himself also rested from his works, as God did from His" (Hebrews 4:9–10). God rested on the seventh day because the work of creation was finished. So too, we can rest in our salvation because the work of Messiah is finished. The Sabbath, according to the writer of Hebrews, depicts God's grace.

When Jewish people keep the Sabbath, they must rest from all forms of prohibited work. In a similar way, when we place faith in Messiah, we rest from striving to earn salvation. We can be confident that the work is finished. We can rest in the certainty of His grace.

THE SABBATH OF GRACE

Like grace itself, God gives the Sabbath as a free gift.

For six days we strive. For six days we try hard. For six days life is about our works and deeds. Six days you shall labor and do all your work to support yourself and your family. For six days we strive to impose our wills onto creation: shaping, creating, forming, making, ordering, structuring, organizing, mixing, and molding—producing results. But on the seventh day, we stop. By stopping for a day, we acknowledge God. By keeping the Sabbath, I acknowledge that it is not by my own hand nor by my own power but by His hand and power that I am sustained. The Sabbath forces me to acknowledge that I am not the creator, the maker, or the shaper. I am not God. I cannot provide for myself through my own effort; He is the one who provides for me.

This is the message of God's grace as well. Though we must strive to be counted worthy, to clear the bar of righteousness, our human failings hamper those efforts and, in the end, we can never be righteous enough to make the grade. Our works of righteousness will never be adequate to merit our own redemption. When salvation comes, we realize the work is over. It is done. God says, "Rest. Enter My rest because the work is done. Not because you finished it; because I finished it. It is already accomplished. Now just rest."

We rest in the perfection of His new creation. We rest in the finished work of His Son. Yeshua said it from the cross: "It is finished" (John 19:30). It is done. There is nothing we can add to it. We can only rest in it. There is nothing we can do to improve on it. Just rest in it.

SABBATH OF FREEDOM

Sometimes we find it hard to rest. We want to shape just one more thing. We want to control just one more thing. We say, "Please God, let me impose my will on just one more thing." Something is on sale at the mall. There is a big game on Saturday. We did not get the roast into the oven. There is overtime available at work.

Sometimes we find it hard to stop and rest because our busy schedules drive us like Pharaoh. "More bricks, more bricks, and get your own darn straw!" Pharaoh says. How can we take a break when we have all these bricks to make? We don't have time.

The commandment of Sabbath forces us to stop for one day and remember. Who created time? Who set time in motion? Who set the spheres revolving? For one day out of a week, the Sabbath reminds us that we serve God, not Pharaoh. We are God's servants. We keep the Sabbath because He has set us free, and as freed men and women, we are able to keep His holy day.

SABBATH OF MESSIAH

If the Sabbath foreshadows things to come and the Sabbath is the substance of Messiah, it stands to reason that the Sabbath pertains to all the disciples of Yeshua. In accordance with Jewish tradition, we initiate and welcome the Sabbath on Friday night with a cup of wine and the breaking of bread, in a manner reminiscent of the table rituals of Passover. Deuteronomy assigns the Sabbath as a remembrance of the exodus from Egypt.[85] In its own small way, every Sabbath is like a little Passover feast, an echo of that moment when Yeshua told us to take the cup and bread in remembrance of Him. In that respect, every meal of the Sabbath can be a meal of remembrance dedicated to the Messiah.

Yeshua is our blessing and holiness, our deep peace, and our sure salvation. He is our new creation, our source of grace and our great freedom. He brings the kingdom—the future Sabbath rest of all creation. He is our Sabbath rest; thus we rest on the Sabbath in Him.

THE SABBATH-BREAKER

"But wait! Jesus was a Sabbath-breaker, wasn't He?"

Well, that's what His enemies among the Pharisees claimed. They said, "This man is not from God, because He does not keep the Sabbath" (John 9:16). His enemies wanted to prove that He was a Sabbath-breaker because, according to the Torah, breaking the Sabbath is a sin. If they could prove that He was a sinner, they could prove that He was not the Messiah.

The same allegation is still being lodged against Yeshua nearly two thousand years later. "Jesus broke the Sabbath!" But this time it is His followers, not His enemies, who accuse Him of Sabbath-breaking. Why are Christians so eager to affirm the Pharisees' allegations?

From a simple reading of the Gospels, it does seem that Yeshua must have been a Sabbath-breaker. His disciples plucked grain on the Sabbath; He defended them. He healed people on the Sabbath. He told a man to carry his mat home on the Sabbath. He made mud and applied it as salve to a blind man's eyes on the Sabbath. All of these constitute legitimate violations of the Sabbath. So what's going on in these stories?

According to Jewish law, the Sabbath can and must be broken if necessary to save life. Yeshua extended that ethic to include the alleviation of human suffering. He taught that showing compassion for human beings takes priority over the ceremonial prohibitions, because God says, "I desire compassion and not a sacrifice" (Matthew 12:7). Just as saving a life takes priority over the Sabbath's prohibitions. He said, "The Sabbath was made for man, and not man for the Sabbath" (Mark 2:27).

Even according to traditional Jewish law, some of the questions Yeshua raised had no clear answers. Two centuries later, the rabbis of the Talmud were still arguing about the conditions under which it might be permissible to heal on the Sabbath, carry a load on the Sabbath, make medicine on the Sabbath, or apply salve on the Sabbath.[86]

SABBATH AND SUNDAY

"But didn't Jesus move the Sabbath to Sunday?"

No. Nowhere in the Bible does it say, or even imply, that Yeshua or His followers met and worshiped on Sunday.

Keeping the Sabbath day is one of the most often-repeated commandments in the Bible. If Messiah or the apostles meant to change the Sabbath, they would have made the change explicit, and they would have provided compelling teaching to explain why this frequently repeated commandment of the Law no longer applies. They did not. Neither Yeshua nor the apostles nor the early disciples of the apostles regarded Sunday as the Sabbath day. It is not in the Bible. The move to Sunday happened after the days of the apostles.

Sometimes teachers try to find Sunday-observance in the Bible by pointing to Acts 20:7, which says, "On the first of the week, when we were gathered together to break bread ..." but this passage refers to a Sabbath-end (Saturday) meal, such as is still practiced in Judaism today. Remember that the biblical day begins in the evening. In Jewish reckoning, the first of the week begins on Saturday night, not Sunday morning.

Devout Jews still gather on Saturday night, at the end of the Sabbath and the beginning of the new week, for a special meal after the Sabbath. In many Chasidic Jewish communities today, disciples of a particular rebbe gather around their teacher on Saturday night to bid farewell to the Sabbath and to welcome the new week with words of Torah. The Troas community in Acts 20 did something similar. The rest of the story bears this out. That's why Paul spoke all night, not all day, and that's why Eutychus fell asleep and out of the window.

Sometimes teachers point to the obscure mention of John walking on the Isle of Patmos on the Lord's Day.[87] "Doesn't that prove that Sunday was regarded as the Lord's Day?" Look closely at the passage. It never mentions Sunday or the first day of the week.

It is not wrong to worship and assemble on Sunday, but Sunday is not the Sabbath, and we should not suppose that the Sunday morning worship service as it currently exists was Yeshua's idea.

YESHUA'S ATTITUDE TOWARD THE SABBATH

If Yeshua did not change the Sabbath, and if Yeshua was not a Sabbath-breaker (and He certainly was not), then what was His attitude toward the Sabbath? When we read the New Testament from a Jewish perspective, it becomes clear that the Sabbath mattered a great deal to Yeshua. Think of how many stories from the Gospels are set on the Sabbath day. Yeshua performed many of His most important miracles on Sabbaths. The Gospels tell us that He went to the synagogue every Sabbath, and that such was His custom.[88] That is because the Sabbath is supposed to be the day of assembly.[89] The Greek word *synagogue* means "assembly." The Gospels depict Yeshua celebrating Sabbath with meals among the Pharisees and spending Sabbath among the disciples.[90] Yeshua regarded the Sabbath as the day of rest, the day of redemption and healing, and the day of His Father. The only work He did on the Sabbath was the work of redemption, the work of His Father.[91] He used it as a day for healing human bodies and souls.

He often knocked heads with religious authorities over how one should keep the Sabbath. The religious authorities of His day were locked into their own heated arguments over how to keep the

Sabbath properly. Yeshua was concerned with restoring a balanced perspective regarding compassion for human beings. His conflict with the Pharisees over the particulars of how one ought to observe the Sabbath shows that the Sabbath was an important institution to Him. Far from dismissing the Sabbath or telling His disciples to disregard it, He was concerned that the Sabbath be kept according to the spirit in which God gave it.

Yeshua told His disciples to pray that their flight from Jerusalem would not take place on a Sabbath day.[92] Even the rabbis allow for one to flee on the Sabbath in order to save one's life, but Yeshua told His disciples to pray that they would not need to break the Sabbath to save their lives. Those do not sound like the words of a Sabbath-breaker.

Yeshua told them, "The Son of Man is Lord of the Sabbath" (Luke 6:5). Would the Lord of the Sabbath not keep the Sabbath? On another occasion He told them, "The Son can do nothing of Himself, unless it is something He sees the Father doing; for whatever the Father does, these things the Son also does in like manner" (John 5:19). This being the case, Yeshua certainly kept the Sabbath. After all, His Father first rested on the Sabbath and declared it blessed and holy.

ACCORDING TO THE COMMANDMENT

If there is any doubt as to what Yeshua taught His disciples regarding the Sabbath, we need only look into the story of His burial. The Gospel of Luke says that the Sabbath was about to begin as the tomb was closed:

> The Sabbath was about to begin. Now the women who had come with Him out of Galilee followed, and saw the tomb and how His body was laid. Then they returned and prepared spices and perfumes. And on the Sabbath they rested according to the commandment. (Luke 23:54–56)

The disciples of Yeshua revered the Sabbath so much that they would not violate it even for the sake of attending to their Master's body. Had Yeshua taught them to disregard the Sabbath, they would not have been concerned with resting "according to the commandment." No trifling concern could have stood between the women and the body of their beloved Teacher. But Yeshua had taught them to revere the Sabbath, and revere it they did. Even though it meant waiting an extra day before they could pay honor to the body of the Master, "on the Sabbath they rested according to the commandment."

A DAY OF REST FOR ALL GOD'S CHILDREN

After His death and resurrection, the community of Yeshua's disciples continued in His ways, and they kept the Sabbath. Some might suppose that only His Jewish followers kept the Sabbath, and that the Gentile believers did not. After all, the apostles made no mention of the Sabbath when they issued the apostolic decree for Gentiles in Acts 15. On the contrary, the first Gentile disciples of Yeshua were also Sabbatarian in that they had no other holy days or days of worship other than the ones the Torah gave them.

Jews and Gentiles have a different relationship to the Sabbath day, but it's the same day for both. Jewish people are obligated to keep the Sabbath and its prohibitions. A Jewish person commits a sin when he neglects to observe the Sabbath. Gentile believers are not obligated in this way. A Gentile believer has not committed a sin if he does not keep the Sabbath's prohibitions. In the days of the apostles, a Jewish person could be punished by the Sanhedrin and, theoretically, incur a death penalty for transgressing the Sabbath. That was not the case for Gentile believers because the Torah does not require Gentiles to observe the Sabbath. Gentile Sabbatarians celebrate the Sabbath and observe some of its prohibitions because they want to, not because they are required to. The Prophet Isaiah tells us that, in the end times, non-Jews who keep the Sabbath day will be given a place in God's holy Temple:

> Also the foreigners who join themselves to the LORD, to minister to Him, and to love the name of the LORD, to be His servants, every one who keeps from profaning the Sabbath and holds fast My covenant; even those I will bring to My holy mountain and make them joyful in My house of prayer. (Isaiah 56:6–7)

Paul's non-Jewish converts met in the synagogues. In Acts 15, James mentions that Gentiles will hear Torah in the synagogues on the Sabbath day.[93] This implies that they were already keeping the Sabbath before the mandates of Acts 15. It also implies that the apostles assumed that they would continue to do so. There was no other day of worship.

The Gospels preserve the numerous stories about Yeshua's healing work on the Sabbath and His arguments regarding the Sabbath because those issues were still relevant to the early believers for whom the Gospels were written. They were Sabbatarians, and they wanted to know what the Master did on the Sabbath. It mattered to them, and that is why those stories are in the Bible.

Unfortunately, when those same stories are read outside the context of a Sabbatarian perspective, we misinterpret them to mean that Yeshua taught against Sabbath-keeping. That misreading plays well into the hands of His detractors. If Yeshua was a Sabbath-breaker, then His enemies among the Pharisees were correct. He was a sinner, and He could not be the Messiah. Our faith is in vain.

He was without sin. Therefore, we know that He kept the Sabbath as the Gospels indicate. He kept the Sabbath and He taught His disciples to keep the Sabbath.

CHAPTER TWELVE

The Festivals of Torah

As Christians, we have all learned that we are children of Abraham. We have learned that we are brothers with King Yeshua, and hence part of a royal family—sons and daughters of God. Yet we have missed so much of the significance of this elevated status. We have mislaid a portion of our inheritance—the Torah and all the ways of the household of God. The things of the Torah tell us about our spiritual family. The Torah is the inheritance of the Jewish believer and the biblical heritage of all the disciples of Yeshua.

GOD'S CALENDAR

In the previous chapter, we learned about the biblical Sabbath, a large component of our lost heritage. The Bible refers to the Sabbath as one of God's appointed times. In this chapter, we will learn about other appointed times on the biblical calendar.

In Leviticus 23, God gives a calendar to the Jewish people. The calendar designates certain days as holy days and special sabbaths. As we saw in the case with the Sabbath, the Torah specifically assigns the Jewish people the responsibility of observing the holy days; Gentiles have a different type of relationship with the festivals. Jewish people are obligated to observe the holy days and their corresponding prohibitions. A Jewish person commits a sin when he neglects to do so. Gentile believers do not share that level of obligation. A Gentile believer has not committed a sin if he does not observe the calendar. At the same time, the festivals on the biblical calendar are the only holy days that the Bible offers to

Jews or Gentiles. The apostles did not create an alternate calendar for non-Jews. In this chapter, we will discover why the biblical festivals are significant for all of Yeshua's disciples.

The biblical calendar runs differently than the one to which we are accustomed. The biblical calendar follows the lunar cycle; that is, it corresponds to the phases of the moon. The waxing and waning cycle of the moon determines the day of the biblical month. The tiny sliver of the new moon indicates the first day of the month, the full moon indicates the middle of the month, and the disappearance of the moon indicates the end of the month.

God declares certain days to be His appointed times. He says, "The LORD's appointed times which you shall proclaim as holy convocations—My appointed times are these" (Leviticus 23:2).

What does this mean? We can understand it if we think about our own busy schedules. Many people keep a day-planner. These contain blank calendars on which to enter various appointments. Today people might use Google Calendar or some other mobile application, but it's the same idea. Suppose you intend to meet your friend Joe at a coffee shop. You and Joe might set a time—say, Tuesday, August 17, at 2:00 PM You would flip open your phone to find the calendar page that shows your schedule for Tuesday, August 17. After you determine that the 2:00 slot is open, you make the entry: "Coffee shop with Joe."

Leviticus 23 functions as God's day-planner. He has made appointments on which to meet with His people. They include the weekly Sabbath, the Festivals of Passover and Pentecost, the Festival of Trumpets, the Day of Atonement, and the Festival of Booths. They are His appointments. Unlike our day-planners and easily deleted entries on Google Calendar, God's day-planner does not change.

When we feel uncertain about whether or not we will be able to keep an appointment, we might say, "I'll pencil it in." This implies that if things change and we are unable to keep the appointment, we can change our plans. God has no uncertainty about His schedule. You might say He doesn't even own a pencil. When He wrote out His day-planner, He wrote in ink, and the ink has been dry for 3,400 years.

PASSOVER AND THE LAMB

After the weekly Sabbath, Leviticus 23 lists Passover as the first appointed time on the calendar. On the first Passover, God told His people to slaughter a lamb and apply its blood to the doorposts of their homes. They were to eat the lamb with bitter herbs and unleavened bread. That night, God rescued them from Egypt and told them to keep the Festival of Passover as a remembrance of their salvation from bondage and slavery. Yet, as God has since revealed, Passover was more than just a remembrance. It also rehearsed something wonderful to come: one of God's appointed times.

Yeshua went with His disciples to keep the Passover in Jerusalem 1,400 years after the exodus from Egypt. He always kept the Father's appointed times; He and His disciples had been to Jerusalem to keep the Passover many times before. But this time was different. Yeshua was about to fulfill the appointed time in a marvelous and unexpected way. As they neared Jerusalem, Yeshua said, "My time is near; I am to keep the Passover" (Matthew 26:18). He kept the Passover Seder meal with His disciples. He took the unleavened bread and the customary Passover cup with His disciples. Christians remember it as the Eucharist or "the Lord's Supper." Then, on the day of Passover, He became the Passover lamb. At the time when Israel slaughtered their Passover lambs in remembrance of their great salvation from Egypt, Yeshua suffered on the cross and His blood was applied as a mark of salvation on all who would believe in Him.

Yeshua's Passover sacrifice gives us a vivid example of how the appointed times work. God uses these times for doing business and for accomplishing the work of redemption. The appointed times teach about the work of Yeshua. Paul told the Corinthians to keep Messiah in mind as they celebrated the Festival of Passover. He reminded us that, just as we cast out the leaven in order to keep the Festival of Unleavened Bread, we also need to cast out the sin that spreads like leaven in our lives:

> Clean out the old leaven so that you may be a new lump, just as you are in fact unleavened. For Messiah our Passover also has been sacrificed. Therefore let us celebrate

the feast, not with old leaven, nor with the leaven of malice and wickedness, but with the unleavened bread of sincerity and truth. (1 Corinthians 5:7–8)

Every year, as my family keeps the Festival of Passover, we do so in remembrance of Yeshua. After all, Messiah Himself told us to keep the Passover in remembrance of Him (Luke 22:19). Did He have in mind only the breaking of bread and drinking of wine? No. He spoke those words within a specific context: Passover. He said, "I have earnestly desired to eat this Passover with you before I suffer; for I say to you, I shall never again eat it until it is fulfilled in the kingdom of God" (Luke 22:15–16).

The commandment to do "this" in remembrance of Yeshua is not a commandment just to take a cup and some bread. The specific "this" to which Yeshua referred was the Passover Seder meal. Not one cup but the traditional cups of Passover. Not any bread but the unleavened matzah bread of Passover. What could be more appropriate for a disciple of Yeshua to do than to keep the Festival of Passover in remembrance of Him, just as He told His disciples?

As believers keeping the Passover, we can use the annual remembrance of our Savior's suffering as a time to renew our lives in Him. We will do well to take the Apostle Paul's advice and "cast out the old leaven," both from our homes and from our lives.

THE BARLEY SHEAF AND THE RESURRECTION

Leviticus 23 identifies the next appointed time on God's calendar as a special day that falls during the seven days of Passover. The Torah tells Israel to bring a sheaf of the first ripened grain to the Temple as a first fruits offering to the LORD. They are to bring it on "the day after the sabbath."[94]

Every disciple of Jesus should be familiar with the command to bring the first sheaf (*omer*) of the harvest to the Temple. This obscure appointment on the biblical calendar—sometimes called the First Fruits of the Barley Harvest, sometimes called First Day of the Omer—is a minor festival with major Messianic implications.

On the same day that Yeshua was tried before the priests and judges of the Sanhedrin, agents from the Sanhedrin went out to a barley field not far from Jerusalem. On the same day that Yeshua was bound and crucified, the agents of the Sanhedrin bound up the standing barley into bundles while it was still attached to the ground so that it would be easier to reap.[95] The day of Yeshua's resurrection, they reaped the barley, collected it, and brought it to Jerusalem for a special first fruits offering to the LORD. According to the Torah, no one could use or eat grain and produce from the new year's crops until a sheaf of the first grain to ripen was harvested and brought to the Temple. Barley is the first crop to ripen in Israel, so the first fruits offering was always a barley sheaf. The commandment of the barley sheaf served to remind Israel that the land and its produce belonged first to God. The produce of the land could not be enjoyed until God had received His due acknowledgement.

By divine design, the ritual of offering the first fruits sheaf in the Temple coincided with the death and resurrection of Yeshua. Perhaps this is what the Apostle Paul had in mind when he declared, "But now Messiah has been raised from the dead, the first fruits of those who are asleep" (1 Corinthians 15:20). Obviously, the celebration of the first fruits of the barley—the day of the resurrection of Messiah—should be important for the disciples of Messiah.

PENTECOST AND THE FIRE ON THE MOUNTAIN

According to Leviticus 23, the next appointment on God's calendar is fifty days after the day the priests offered the sheaf of barley grain in the Temple. We call it the Festival of Pentecost because Pentecost means "fifty." Judaism refers to it as the Festival of Weeks (*Shavu'ot*) because it occurs seven weeks after Passover.

Long before the day of Pentecost became a Christian holiday, the Jewish sages considered Pentecost to be the anniversary of the day God spoke the Torah at Mount Sinai. Judaism calls it the festival of the "Giving of the Torah." Before tongues of fire ever fell upon the believers in Jerusalem, fire fell on Mount Sinai. As the disciples of the risen Messiah gathered to celebrate Pentecost in Jerusalem, they gathered to celebrate the anniversary of the giving of the Torah.

Let's consider the significance of the first Pentecost at Mount Sinai. Exodus 19–20 tells the story. God stepped down from the heavens; His presence rested on the top of a mountain. The people saw lightning, fire, and smoke. They heard thunder and the loud sound of a ram's horn trumpet blowing. The earth shook. The entire nation audibly heard the voice of God speaking the Ten Commandments.

According to Jewish legend, when God spoke the Ten Commandments on Mount Sinai, His voice spoke in all the languages of mankind, and took the shape of fiery sparks that encircled the camp of Israel and came to rest on each individual Jew.[96]

Is that how it really happened? Perhaps God's voice did speak in every language. Perhaps it did not. Perhaps His words came forth as fiery sparks that rested on each individual. Perhaps they did not. Just remember that Peter and the disciples and followers of Yeshua were all familiar with the Pentecost legends. They must have known the story of the giving of the Torah on Pentecost. They knew the story of the words of fire resting on each individual. They knew the story of God's voice speaking to all mankind in every language. Therefore, the miracles, signs, and wonders that came upon them during that extraordinary Pentecost carried deep significance. The apostles would have understood the appearance of tongues of fire and the miraculous gift of speaking in unknown languages as directly parallel the Mount Sinai experience and the receiving of the Torah.

God, through these unmistakable and miraculous parallels, drew a line of connection between the giving of His Torah and the giving of His Spirit. We cannot see one without considering the other. The two events reveal a close relationship between God's Spirit and His Law.

If we believe that God's Spirit plays a role of any importance in the life of the believer, then it should go without saying that the Festival of Pentecost is relevant to the disciples of Messiah. Just as the disciples gathered together for Pentecost, and Paul hurried across the Mediterranean to arrive in Jerusalem for Pentecost, so should we be eager to keep this appointed time. [97]

ROSH HASHANAH: THE FESTIVAL OF TRUMPETS

Leviticus 23 lists more important appointments on God's calendar: the fall holidays of the Festival of Trumpets, the Day of Atonement, and the Festival of Booths. The Torah tells the Jewish people to celebrate the Festival of Trumpets by blowing a ram's horn trumpet (*shofar*). The sound of the trumpet prepares us for the holy Day of Atonement that comes ten days later. The trumpet reminds us to repent. Jewish tradition identifies the Festival of Trumpets as the New Year (*Rosh HaShanah*), a day for reconciling with friends and families, setting aside differences, and asking for forgiveness. It's a day for repenting. We use the turning of the calendar at Rosh HaShanah to review the previous year's sins and shortcomings, and we make a special effort to apologize to one another and forgive one another.

Rosh HaShanah reminds us of the appointed time yet to come when the Master "will send forth His angels with a great trumpet and they will gather together His elect from the four winds, from one end of the sky to the other" (Matthew 24:31). On Rosh HaShanah, we anticipate the coming judgment, the trumpets of the book of Revelation, and the beginning of the end. It offers us a glimpse of the future to come, a shadow cast through time. As such, Rosh HaShanah is relevant for everyone who believes in Messiah's return.

THE DAY OF ATONEMENT

The next appointed time on God's calendar occurs ten days after Rosh HaShanah. It is the Day of Atonement (*Yom Kippur*). The Bible says, "It is on this day that atonement shall be made for you to cleanse you; you will be clean from all your sins before the LORD" (Leviticus 16:30). The Day of Atonement is the holiest day of the year. Its exalted holiness arises from the fact that it marks the anniversary of the day on which the holiest man in the world used to enter the holiest place in the world. The holiest man in the world was the high priest of Israel. The holiest place was the holy of holies in the Temple. Every year, on the Day of Atonement, the high priest used to enter the holy of holies to apply the atoning blood of the sin offerings.

According to apostolic teaching, the Day of Atonement teaches us about the work of Messiah on our behalf. He is our High Priest—not in the Temple on earth, but in the heavenly Temple. He carried His own atoning blood into the holy of holies of the heavenly Temple (so to speak).

Jewish custom refers to the Day of Atonement as Judgment Day because of its biblical associations with sin, atonement, and forgiveness. The traditional synagogue Day of Atonement service lasts most of the day, and encompasses several long prayer services. Since it is a fast day, the community spends the whole day in prayer, confession, study, and reflection. Most Messianic Jewish communities spend the day together and break the fast together at the end of the day. The Day of Atonement has special significance for disciples of Yeshua because it is the day we rehearse Yeshua's work on our behalf. On this, the holiest day of the year, we concern ourselves with the cleansing, atoning work of Messiah that has wrought for us forgiveness, pardon, and right standing with God. Prayers of confession are a key component. The Gospels and the Epistles frequently enjoin us to confess our sins. The Day of Atonement sets aside twenty-five hours for deliberate, intentional, and conscientious confession of sin. It is a twenty-five-hour period of devotional introspection during which we scrutinize our behavior, confess our shortcomings, and throw ourselves on the mercy and grace of our great King. Spending the Day of Atonement among believers who take the day seriously is an amazing, life-changing experience, something relevant for every disciple of Messiah.

THE FESTIVAL OF BOOTHS (FESTIVAL OF TABERNACLES)

Leviticus 23 lists the Festival of Booths as the last appointment on God's calendar, an eight-day harvest celebration. The Hebrew name of the festival is *Sukkot*, a word that means "shelters, booths, or huts." The word refers to temporary, tent-like structures, sometimes translated as "tabernacles" in English Bibles. The festival is so named because the Torah commands the Jewish people to annually build and live in temporary booths during the seven days of the festival as a reminder of the huts and booths in which they lived in the wilderness after leaving Egypt.[98]

Judaism adorns Sukkot with beautiful traditions. For example, it is traditional to invite guests into one's booth for a festive meal each night of the festival. Prominent on the guest list are some auspicious names: Abraham, Isaac, Jacob, Joseph, Moses, Aaron, and David. Each one is specially invited to come into the booth and pull up a chair at the table during one of the days of the festival. Obviously, Abraham, Isaac, Jacob, Joseph, Moses, Aaron, and David are unlikely to actually attend the meal, since they are all dead. That, however, is the point of the ritual. Sukkot anticipates the Messianic Age when the dead will be raised to life again and we will all sit at table with the aforementioned in the kingdom of heaven. In that day, each man will take shelter under his own vine and fig tree.[99] A sukkah of glory will be spread over Jerusalem.[100] According to the prophets, the Festival of Booths celebrates a time when all nations will ascend to Jerusalem bearing tribute to King Messiah and celebrating the festival:

> Then it will come about that any who are left of all the nations that went against Jerusalem will go up from year to year to worship the King, the LORD of hosts, and to celebrate the Feast of Booths. (Zechariah 14:16)

I like to make a case for placing the birth of Yeshua during Sukkot. I know of one source that suggests Jewish believers used to celebrate the first day of Sukkot as the day of Messiah's birth.[101] The Gospel of John gives us a hint too. The Apostle John uses a verb form of the same Greek word that the Greek Bible used to translate the word *sukkah* when he wrote, "And the Word became flesh, and dwelt [tabernacled] among us" (John 1:14). He tabernacled among us then, and He will tabernacle among us again in the Messianic Era.

The Festival of Booths celebrates the Messiah who once tabernacled among us, now tabernacles within us, and in the future will again tabernacle among us. In that day, all nations will ascend to His throne in Jerusalem in order to celebrate the festival.

SHADOWS OF MESSIAH

When we look over the appointed times on God's calendar, it is easy to see Messiah in each appointment. This is what Paul meant when he said that the festivals are shadows of things to come and the substance of Messiah.

APPOINTED TIME	MESSIANIC MEANING
Sabbath (*Shabbat*) Leviticus 23:2–3	Sabbath rest of creation; the final redemption; the Messianic Era
Passover (*Pesach*) Leviticus 23:4–8	The Last Supper; Messiah our Passover Lamb; Yeshua's death and burial
First Fruits of the Barley (*Omer*) Leviticus 23:9–14	Messiah's resurrection
Pentecost (*Shavu'ot*) Leviticus 23:15–21	The giving of the Torah at Sinai; the outpouring of the Spirit
Festival of Trumpets (*Rosh HaShanah*) Leviticus 23:23–25	The trumpet blast of the return of Messiah; the call to repentance.
Day of Atonement (*Yom Kippur*) Leviticus 23:26–32	The atoning work of Messiah's sacrifice; the day of final judgment.
The Festival of Booths (*Sukkot*) Leviticus 23:33–44	Sabbath rest of creation; the Messianic Era, the birth of the Messiah

Paul told the Gentile believers of the city of Colossae:

> Let no one, then, judge you in eating or in drinking, or in respect of a feast, or of a new moon, or of sabbaths, which are a shadow of the coming things, and the body [is] of the Messiah. (Colossians 2:16–17, Young's Literal Translation)

Some versions of the Bible display their translators' biases. For example, the NASB inserts the word "mere" into the verse in order to diminish the importance of the biblical festivals. It then reads, "things which are a *mere* shadow of what is to come; but the substance belongs to Christ," implying that the festivals and laws of Torah are insubstantial and inconsequential. The New International Version translators changed the tense of the verb to the past tense so that it reads, "These are a shadow of the things that *were* to come; the reality, however, is found in Christ."

The literal reading of the verse does not set Messiah and the things of Torah in antithesis, nor does it dismiss the matters of Torah as irrelevant relics of the past. Paul tells the Colossian believers that the true relevance of the biblical calendar (new moons) and the biblical Sabbaths and festivals, and their celebration (eating and drinking), is that they are shadows of coming things and the substance (literally "body") of Messiah.

The metaphor is clear enough. Every shadow results from a shadow-caster. Messiah is the body; the biblical calendar is the shadow He casts. Paul told the Colossians not to allow people to judge them in regard to things that are substantially about Messiah. Paul encouraged the Colossians not to allow ascetics to judge them for celebrating the Sabbath and the biblical festivals with food and drink.

At any rate, we should not read this passage as a dismissal of the value of keeping the festivals. Instead Paul tells us that they are a shadow of things to come and the substance of Messiah. If anything, he encourages us to see the true meaning of the festivals. When we realize that the substance of the appointed times is Messiah, we are more inclined to keep them. It becomes a matter of discipleship.

God's calendar does more than point to the Messiah; it actually changes our lives. It creates a cycle of sanctification, an annual pattern of growth for healthy discipleship. Every Passover we are to recount Israel's salvation and relive the dramatic redemption that is ours in Messiah our Passover Lamb. On Pentecost we retell the story of the revelation at Sinai and we relive the vivifying reception of the Holy Spirit. On Rosh HaShanah we tremble in anticipation of Messiah's return and prepare our hearts for that final judgment by exercising heartfelt repentance, confession, and reconciliation. On the Day of Atonement we cast ourselves on God's grace as we confess that we are unworthy of His mercy, but gratefully accept the free gift of His pardon and atonement. On the Festival of Sukkot we celebrate God's bounty upon us and rejoice over the work He has accomplished in our lives over the course of the year as we eagerly look forward to the kingdom when Messiah will once more tabernacle among us.

As the disciples of the Messiah rediscover the biblical festivals, we rediscover our own spiritual heritage and reclaim our spiritual identity.

CHAPTER THIRTEEN

The Life of Torah

Imagine a man on a long journey, exiled from his home and in search of a new land. On his back he carries all of his belongings. He bears a great load, but his back is strong and his legs are stout. As he travels, bandits waylay him. In order to escape them, he tosses some of his belongings aside. The lighter load allows him to move faster. Some time later, when he has run out of money, he finds he must barter certain items for food for the journey. On another occasion he inadvertently leaves some precious items behind at a lodging place, not noticing the loss until much later. When his long journey is finally complete, he has lost along the way most of the belongings with which he originally set out.

That's the story of Christianity and the Torah. Christianity set out from Jerusalem two thousand years ago on a long journey into all nations. Along the way, we lost many of the things that once were precious to us. Among the things we left at various stages on our journey were the celebration of the Sabbath and the biblical festivals. In this chapter, we will consider a few other examples of lost items that need to be restored to the disciples of Yeshua.

THE CYCLE OF PRAYER

The earliest Christians prayed three times a day every day. We inherited that routine from Judaism. Jewish tradition prescribes three times of prayer daily: morning, afternoon, and evening. The Prophet Daniel prayed "toward Jerusalem ... three times a day, praying and giving thanks before his God" (Daniel 6:10).

The times of prayer correspond to the times of sacrifice that took place in the Temple: "Peter and John were going up to the temple at the ninth hour, the hour of prayer" (Acts 3:1). Yeshua's Jewish disciples dedicated themselves to "the prayers," worshiping continually in the Temple and synagogues, in concert with the liturgical cycle. Likewise, early Gentile Christians prayed the Lord's Prayer three times a day, presumably at the Jewish hours of prayer.[102]

Christian tradition retains the Jewish times of prayer. The times of prayer are still observed in liturgical forms of Christianity like the Roman Catholic confession and the Orthodox confession. Many Protestants, however, have never heard of the ancient discipline that once defined the daily devotion of believers.

The discipline of daily prayer at the times of prayer could be an asset to all believers and should be restored to Yeshua's disciples. In Messianic Judaism today, many disciples of Yeshua observe the practice of daily prayer at the prescribed times. Messianic Jewish believers even use the prescribed prayers of Jewish liturgy to add their "amen" to the petitions of the synagogue.[103]

THE MONTHLY CYCLE

On our journey from Jerusalem, we lost the biblical calendar. Believers in Yeshua used to follow the Jewish calendar for determining the months, seasons, and holy days because the Jewish calendar is the biblical calendar. Every month, the phases of the moon mark out the passing days according to its waxing and waning. As we watch the moon grow to its fullness and recede until it vanishes from the sky, it teaches us important truths about God's rhythms and cycles.

In Judaism, when the new moon appears, it is said to be "born again," a monthly reminder of spiritual rebirth and the coming redemption.

Judaism points out an obvious connection between the monthly cycle of the moon and the monthly cycle of the human body. God has synchronized the body of the typical woman to approximate the lunar month; so long as her menstrual cycle is regular, she will begin her cycle at the same phase of the moon each month. Human beings are synchronized to the moon. A woman's body is uniquely tuned to God's calendar, practicing a continual cycle of rebirth and re-creation.

During a woman's week of menstruation, the Torah designates her as Levitically "unclean." That sounds nasty. A better translation would be "unfit." In the Torah, a person might be either ritually clean (*tahor*) or ritually unclean (*tamei*). The problem with the English words clean and unclean is that they seem to imply that there is something dirty, repulsive, shameful, or morally deficient about a person who is "unclean." That is not the case.

We could avoid these unfortunate and inaccurate connotations by translating the Hebrew terms *tahor* and *tamei* as "ritually fit" and "ritually unfit" respectively. To be ritually fit is to be in a state whereby a person is fit to enter the Temple, participate in its services, and eat of the sacrifices. A ritually unfit person is barred from admission and is required to abstain from eating the sacrifices. It is not a sin to be ritually unfit, but it is a sin to eat of the sacrifices while ritually unfit.

UNCLEAN (*tamei*): A ceremonial state in which a person is unfit to enter the Temple or eat of the sacrifices.

CLEAN (*tahor*): A ceremonial state in which a person is fit to enter the Temple and eat of the sacrifices.

In actual practice today, a woman's monthly uncleanness has no real relevance because there is no Temple. If the Temple still stood, she would not be able to enter the Temple or eat of the sacrifices until menstruation ended and she went through a ceremonial purification. To become ritually clean after menstruation, a woman need only immerse herself in a ritual baptism.

Even without a Temple, menstruation is still an important matter of concern in the Torah. God expressly prohibits sexual relations for seven days after menstruation begins.[104] (Just to be safe, Jewish tradition reckons it as seven days after the cycle ends.) This is a matter of sexual morality aside from any ritual purity concerns. Abstinence during menstruation is one of the Bible's laws of sexual morality, just like the prohibitions on incest and homosexuality.

This law applies to both Jews and Gentiles because the apostles specifically included the prohibition on sexual immorality in the apostolic decree of Acts 15. The laws pertaining to menstruation are called the laws of family purity.

In Jewish communities, married women still practice a monthly ritual immersion as a remembrance of the way things were in the Temple age. Her immersion marks the end of the period of abstinence engendered by menstruation. Husband and wife may resume sexual contact with one another after the woman's immersion. Families that practice the laws of family purity describe this reunion as a monthly honeymoon.

A woman's body, like the moon, depicts a continual process of renewal and rebirth. Each month, a woman's body passes from life to death to life again. She passes from ritual, Levitical uncleanness to Levitical purity through the rite of immersion.

Messiah Himself is our baptism. The apostles say that we are baptized into His death and resurrection. In Him we are purified and renewed, born again like the moon, like the woman cleansed and returned to her husband. In this way the Torah elevates the woman's monthly cycle from the level of the mundane and normal to a level of holiness, spiritual truth, and transformation.

The synchronicity of the human menstrual cycle and the lunar cycle teaches us about our connection to the biblical calendar. Our bodies are tuned to God's calendar.

BAPTISM

When a woman immerses herself for purification, she does so in a special immersion pool called a mikvah. The laws of the mikvah and ceremonial immersion are the origin of the Christian sacrament of baptism.

Many Christians are surprised to learn that ritual baptism was practiced in Judaism long before the days of John the Baptist. They may also be surprised to learn that ritual baptism is still practiced today among traditional Jews. Christianity did not invent baptism.

Baptism originally began as a purification ritual in the days of Moses, but according to Jewish apocrypha, even Adam and Eve immersed themselves in the Euphrates River to symbolize their penitence after being expelled from the garden.

Christians generally have different ideas about how baptism should be done and what it means. Once, when I was conducting a Torah class at a small Bible study group, I brought up the issue of baptism. We discussed the origin of the ritual in Jewish practice. Everyone was fascinated. Then I asked the students, "From what denomination of Christianity do you each come?" We had three Lutherans, an Evangelical, two Catholics, a Baptist, and a Methodist in attendance that night. I said, "Isn't this amazing? We all come from different denominations with different ideas about baptism. In fact, baptism is one of the subjects that most deeply divides us. But here we are, all learning together about baptism. That's the beauty of discovering our Jewish roots: Torah is something we all have in common, since it is older than the theologies that divide us now. It is our common origin."

In the days of the apostles, Jews practiced ritual baptism frequently, sometimes daily. From the days of Moses, all Israel had regularly participated in ritual purification immersions. Anyone who became ritually unclean needed to undergo an immersion before they could enter the Temple. The priests immersed every day. After a woman completed menstruation, she needed to immerse herself before she could rejoin her husband or participate in the Temple. Those who had become contaminated in any way (e.g., lepers) needed to go through immersion before they were deemed ritually pure again. In Judaism, immersions like this are referred to as immersion into a mikvah. *Mikvah* is a Hebrew word meaning "gathering of water." A mikvah could be a river, a lake, a spring, or any naturally fed gathering of water. More frequently, however, the Jewish people use pools created specifically for immersions. Ritual immersion in a mikvah comprises a regular part of Jewish life.

MIKVAH: A pool or gathering of water fit for ceremonial purification through immersion.

The Torah forbids anyone from entering into the Temple of God while in a state of ritual impurity, and the only way to be certain of one's ritual purity is to pass through a mikvah.[105] Worshipers going up to the Temple immersed themselves before entering. Modern-day visitors to Jerusalem can see the archaeological remains of these immersion pools all around the Temple Mount and all over Jerusalem. The three thousand new believers the apostles baptized on the day of Pentecost almost certainly immersed themselves in the mikvah facilities around the Temple Mount. The mikvah is a regular feature of Jewish archaeological sites. Immersion baths can be found on Masada, at the Herodium, at Qumran, and all over the land of Israel.

According to Jewish tradition, a Gentile who wants to become Jewish must participate in several ritual ceremonies. Males require both circumcision and immersion. For a woman, immersion constitutes the entire conversion ritual. In Jewish law, a Gentile who converts to Judaism does not legally take on Jewish identity until he comes up out of the water of the mikvah. As such, immersion into a baptismal pool is the final ritual of conversion; it completes the process. Going down into the water, the convert is said to die to his old life. As he comes up, he becomes like a newborn child: a new creature. Gentiles who pass through the immersion pool are symbolically said to be reborn as Jews (or "born again" as Jews, if you prefer).

In the New Testament, the baptism ritual followed the same rubrics and symbolized the same type of spiritual transformation.[106] Jewish believers immersed themselves in a mikvah in the name of Yeshua to identify with Him and declare their allegiance to Him as a disciple. New Gentile disciples also immersed in the mikvah in Yeshua's name.

REMINDERS

The Torah fills life with daily, weekly, monthly, and annual reminders of God. Numbers 15:38–40 refers to one of the daily reminders found in the Torah:

> They shall make for themselves tassels on the corners of their garments throughout their generations … to look at and remember all the commandments of the LORD, so as to do them and not follow after your own heart and

> your own eyes, after which you played the harlot, so that you may remember to do all My commandments and be holy to your God. (Numbers 15:38–40)

The tassels (*tzitzit*) consist of four sets of knots and strings that hang from the corners of the ritual prayer shawl, as well as from a smaller ritual garment worn underneath one's shirt. Even the Master wore these tassels; in fact, they became an important component of His healing ministry.[107]

The commandment of the tassels works in two directions. First, the Jewish person wearing the tassels is reminded that he represents God in the world. The tassels symbolize the commandments; by wearing the tassels, a Jewish man accepts responsibility for keeping the commandments. Second, people who see him wearing the tassels are reminded of God. They will hold that individual to a higher level of accountability. The tassels are a conspicuous sign of Jewish identity. In that respect, they are similar to the Jesus-fish American Christians often put on their cars. Drivers with the Jesus-fish on their cars are conspicuous. The symbol reminds them to be more godly on the road, and it reminds other drivers of Jesus.

That's the whole idea of the Torah life. God designed everything in the Torah to remind the Jewish people of who they are. From the clothes He commands His people to wear to the food He commands them to eat to the days He commands them to celebrate—He gave Israel all these laws to remind the Jewish people that they are His covenant people.

Many of the Torah's reminders are explicitly stated as such. For example, the weekly Sabbath reminds the Jewish people of their freedom from Egypt and serves as a sign of the covenant between God and Israel. The Passover reminds the Jewish people of the exodus from Egypt; it is a remembrance of salvation and redemption. Other aspects of Torah are not explicitly referred to as "remembrances," but together they form a comprehensive lifestyle that never lets a Jewish person forget who God is or who he or she is.

Here's another example: the *mezuzah*.[108] *Mezuzah* is the Hebrew word for "doorframe"; the commandment of *mezuzah* tells the Jewish people to write God's commandments on the doorframes of their houses.[109] Traditional Jews keep this commandment by affixing a small scroll case (called a *mezuzah*) containing the relevant passage of Scripture onto the doorframes of their homes. The mezuzah identifies the home as a Jewish home and a home that is under the jurisdiction of God's Word. Upon entering and exiting the home, the observant Jew reverently touches the scroll case to remind him of his obligation to be a godly person inside and outside the home.

Similarly, the Torah commands the Jewish people to bind on God's Word: "You shall bind them as a sign on your hand and they shall be as frontals on your forehead" (Deuteronomy 6:8). Jewish men keep this commandment by strapping leather boxes (*tefillin*) containing relevant passages of Scripture to their hands and foreheads during morning prayer.[110] This ancient custom was universal among the mainstream of observant Jews of Yeshua's day. He Himself practiced the commandment. Starting each day with a ceremony in which the Word of God is literally strapped to your head and tied onto your arm creates a powerful reminder. The daily, weekly, monthly, and annual reminders of Torah never give a Jewish person an opportunity to forget who they are.

The Torah's reminders of Jewish identity are not commandments that apply directly to Gentiles. There's nothing at all wrong with observing these things, and many Gentiles in the Messianic movement do so. When I first learned about the Torah, I was eager to wear a tallit, put up a mezuzah, and wrap tefillin just like everyone else. For many years I did, but I found that when Gentile disciples of Yeshua adopt Jewish identity markers, it confuses everyone, including the Gentile disciple. It makes others think that he is Jewish, and it makes the Gentile think of himself as the same as a Jew. For that reason, I now choose not to observe these particular identity-marking commandments.

Nevertheless, Gentile disciples will do well to learn from those commandments and to apply the spiritual principles that they symbolize. Gentile disciples should be encouraged to live conspicuously godly lives, which includes dressing in a godly manner, marking their homes with the word of God, and binding the Scriptures to their heads (what we think about) and to their hands (what we do).

GOD'S COOKBOOK

Among the things that Christianity lost along the way are the biblical dietary laws. In the Torah, God gives His people laws about what they can eat and what they cannot eat. Some of these laws apply to everyone (the laws of Noah). Some of these laws apply to Gentile disciples of Yeshua (the laws of the apostolic decree in Acts 15). Some apply specifically to the Jewish people (the dietary laws of Leviticus 11 and Deuteronomy 14). Some apply only to the priesthood (the laws of sacrifices and sacred gifts).

In Christianity, several key passages of the New Testament have been misunderstood to imply that God's dietary laws no longer apply to anyone. These passages are fully explored and explained in other resources.[111] Suffice it to say that Yeshua kept the dietary laws, as did all the apostles. This being the case, we followers of Yeshua should, at the very least, know something about those laws.

MENU OPTIONS FOR SONS OF NOAH

The average person on planet Earth has a wide range of menu options. As explained earlier, the Torah's only rule for the sons of Noah is a prohibition on eating things while they are still alive. The LORD commanded Noah: "Every moving thing that is alive shall be food for you; I give all to you, as I gave the green plant. Only you shall not eat flesh with its life, that is, its blood" (Genesis 9:3–4). Presumably cannibalism is also off-limits since people are not included in the definition of the Hebrew word for "moving thing." In other words, people are not food.

THE JEWISH DIET

Jews have a much more limited menu. The Torah prohibits Jewish people from eating certain kinds of animals. Leviticus 11 distinguishes between two types of animals: the clean (*tahor*) and the unclean (*tamei*). Jewish people are commanded not to eat the unclean ones. The distinction between clean and unclean animals did not originate in Leviticus or the Sinai covenant. Noah knew the difference between clean and unclean animals even before the flood.[112] The distinction probably reflects an animal's eligibility for sacrifice. Of those animals that were suitable for sacrifice, Noah took seven pairs into the ark. Of those that were not, he took only one pair.

Among all the mammals, God considers only those that both ruminate (chew the cud) and have a split hoof as permissible for Jewish people. These animals are herbivores, and are characterized by their four stomach compartments and two-toed hooves. Examples include cattle, sheep, goats, buffalo, ibex, gazelle, deer, wild ox, and giraffe. The Torah designates mammals that do not possess these characteristics as unclean and unsuitable for Jewish consumption.

The Torah permits fish possessing both fins and scales. Other seafood is not permitted. Shrimp, lobsters, clams, oysters, and the like are all outside the category of permissible seafood for Jews. Furthermore, many fish are regarded as unclean because they lack fins or proper scales. Whales, sharks, eels, and the like are eliminated along with any other fish without scales.

As for fowl, the Torah disqualifies birds of prey and carrion. The following birds are regarded as clean: pigeon, turtle dove, palm dove, hen, chicken, turkey, quail, partridge, peacock, pheasant, sparrow, duck, and goose. The ostrich is among the forbidden birds that might commonly be mistaken as food. The eggs of unclean birds are also unclean.

With the exception of certain types of locusts, grasshoppers, and perhaps crickets, the Bible forbids all insects.

In additional to all these prohibitions, the Torah forbids Jewish people from eating blood, from eating the meat of an animal that died of itself, from eating the meat of an animal that died from any method other than ritual slaughter (i.e., the meat of strangled animals), from meat containing the sciatic nerve, from certain fats, and from meat cooked in milk (from which Jewish law derives the separation of meat and dairy).

FOOD RULES FOR GENTILE BELIEVERS

Gentile disciples are not held to quite the same rigorous standard to which Jewish believers are held. As explained earlier, the apostles prohibited the Gentile disciples "from things sacrificed to idols and from blood and from things strangled" (Acts 15:29).[113] At a minimum, these prohibitions require Gentiles to avoid blood, food tainted by idolatry, and meat that was not properly slaughtered by Jewish standards. Many Gentile believers choose to take on more than just that minimum standard. The *Didache* (a first-century, Apostolic-era catechism for new Gentile disciples) recommends that Gentile believers, while not technically obligated to do so, should consider voluntarily adopting Jewish dietary standards:

> Concerning food, bear what you can, but scrupulously guard yourself from what has been offered to idols, because it is the worship of dead gods. (*Didache* 6:2–3)

Sometimes people try to connect the Bible's dietary laws with healthy nutrition standards, but the biblical dietary laws teach something more than just good health sense. The dietary laws teach us about the difference between the permissible and the forbidden, light and dark, right and wrong.

The first prohibition God gave to mankind was a dietary law. Though He permitted man to eat of any other tree in the garden, He forbade them one tree. The biblical dietary laws bring us back to the garden. They remind us that we are not the authors of morality. God makes the distinctions. It's not a matter of how we feel about a particular thing that makes it wrong or right. So too, with sexual temptations, avarice, and a host of other appetites that tempt our mortal inclinations.

The prophets often used the biblical distinctions between clean and unclean as metaphors for good and evil. Keeping the biblical dietary laws forces us to analyze everything before we put it in our mouths. This basic discipline teaches us to be careful about the things that go into our ears and eyes as well. If we should be careful to avoid eating something that might be deemed ceremonially unfit, how much more so should we be careful to avoid looking at something spiritually unclean or listening to something unwholesome?

THE BEAUTY OF TORAH LIFE

The life of Torah is walked out in quiet beauty and subtle majesty. Until it is experienced, it cannot be understood. Words fall short of explaining. For example, try to explain to someone how your life changed after having met the Master. You might stammer out various external things, but those are only the outward results of something that has happened on the inside. The Christian life is much more than simply changing our behavior. It's about being a new person on the inside, enjoying a relationship with God, the filling of the Holy Spirit, and having the confidence that comes from being able to call God "Abba—Father."

Similarly, from the outside, the Torah life appears to be a matter of external things: certain holy days, a particular diet, and various laws. But these are only external manifestations of something much deeper.

Throughout the day, week, month, and year, the Almighty offers us a regular rhythm of godliness. The Torah mode of life provides daily prayers and constant reminders. When we arise, we pray. When we eat, we bless. When we go in and out, we note the mezuzah on the door. His Word is on our lips when we lie down and when we get up and when we sit in our homes and when we go on the way.[114] As the week commences, we mark off the days until Sabbath, eagerly anticipating a day off from the mundane, a day with the family, a day with friends, and a day with the Master.

Ideally, the Sabbath preparations start on Thursday with extra groceries and dinner plans. On Friday the house is full of activity and good smells. Friday night the soft glow of candles lights the table while songs, prayers, blessings, laughter, and conversation light up the heart. On Saturday night, we gather with friends to bid the Sabbath farewell and begin the countdown to the next Sabbath.

As the weeks pass, the phases of the moon wax and wane, marking off the biblical months, one after another, marching us toward the appointed times of God's festivals. At Passover season, we clean the house to remove the leaven and prepare for the big event. Imagine reading the story of Passover to your children on Passover. Imagine reading them the story of that fateful Passover when the nails pierced our Master's hands and feet. Imagine annually reliving the Last Supper with a simple Passover meal in your home during which you and your family take the cup and the unleavened bread together in remembrance of the Master. Imagine telling the story of the empty tomb as part of your celebration of the ensuing days of the festival.

Soon we are counting the days until Pentecost. Anticipation grows with each passing day. On the fiftieth day we wake up early to attend the special festival service and hear the Ten Commandments read aloud alongside the story of Acts 2. We receive a small taste of the outpouring of the Spirit. Imagine straining to hear the sound of the Master's trumpet while you listen to the ram's horn trumpet blown on Rosh HaShanah, the Festival of Trumpets. Imagine rehearsing the weighty work of Messiah's atonement, confessing your sins in tearful prayers, as you fast through the solemn Day of Atonement.

Five days later, the Festival of Booths finds us in the backyard, building a makeshift hut in which we will eat our meals together throughout the eight days of the festival. Imagine sitting outside in your little booth with family and friends, reading together the gospel story of the Savior's birth, on a cool October evening while the radiant face of the full moon rises over you. Imagine knowing that, in the same way, Yeshua and the apostles once sat in similar booths on the Mount of Olives during the Festival of Booths under the same full moon. At the conclusion of the Festival of Booths, we start the whole cycle over again. Isn't that how it should be for disciples of Yeshua?

On the other hand, the thought of all that might feel overwhelming. Don't be discouraged. You don't have to try to take on everything all at once. Just take one step at a time. Every step toward God and His Word is a step in the right direction.

THE ROAD FROM JERUSALEM

How did we lose all these things?

The interpretation of the New Testament, like any piece of literature, depends upon understanding its context. When we read it outside of its context, we find ourselves unable to interpret it or assess its original meaning. Unfortunately for us, shortly after the age of the apostles came to a close, Judaism and Christianity began their great divorce. The political upheaval of the first and second Jewish Revolts, coupled with Roman state-sponsored persecution, forced non-Jewish believers to disassociate themselves from Judaism. At the same time, believers began to experience concentrated persecution within the synagogues and were actually expelled from participation in the Jewish congregation.

As a result, many Gentile believers in Yeshua were left trying to interpret the Bible with only a superficial knowledge of the original matrix from which it had come. They began to read the New Testament with a decidedly anti-Jewish posture, and interpreted the arguments of the Apostolic-age communities as if they were anti-Jewish and anti-Torah arguments. They quickly forgot that Yeshua, the apostles, and all the early believers were practicing Jews.

In the early second century, Marcion the Heretic led a popular uprising within Christianity with the aim of completely removing the Old Testament (and most of the New Testament as well). He wanted a total disassociation from Judaism.

While Marcion was eventually excommunicated, his theology was not formed in a vacuum; indeed, the Christian church took shape by defining itself in antithesis to Judaism. Within a few centuries, Christians began to consider it a service to God to persecute and kill the Jewish people.

In today's world, the horror of the Nazi Holocaust has shocked us to our senses. We are going back to our Bibles, digging into church history, and researching Jewish sources as we ask ourselves, "How could we have let this happen?" This searching has yielded some surprises. Like archaeologists digging through layers of rubble to find the foundations of the original city, we have begun to clear away years of misinterpretation and anti-Semitic theology. It is exciting work. Among the ancient treasures we have unearthed in this theological, archaeological dig is the Torah itself.

CHAPTER FOURTEEN

The Jots and Tittles of Torah

We are peering through the lattice of King Solomon's palace. Seated upon the massive throne of ivory and gold and lions and precious stones sits King Solomon himself. The rich smell of cedar panels mingles with the fragrance of perfumes. Our eyes take in silks and delicacies and other things tantalizing to the senses. Around the throne servants hurry and fuss to anticipate every need and whim of the king: Solomon in all of his splendor!

KING SOLOMON'S PALACE

But what is the king doing? Two priests stand before him holding aloft a scroll of Torah rolled open to the book of Deuteronomy. Spread across Solomon's throne is another roll of parchment over which the king hunches, pen and ink in hand. He is copying a Torah scroll to fulfill the special commandment for the king to write a copy of the Torah.

The commandment for the king to write a copy of the Torah appears in Deuteronomy 17. By amazing coincidence, Deuteronomy 17 happens to be the chapter of Torah that Solomon is working on as we spy on him. Even now he is beginning to transcribe the special section of laws that apply to the king.

Therein it is written, "Now it shall come about when he sits on the throne of his kingdom, he shall write for himself a copy of this law on a scroll in the presence of the Levitical priests" (Deuteronomy 17:18). God commands the king to write a copy of the Torah. This provision ensures that the king himself submits to the rule of law and does not become a despot without accountability or boundary. Specifically, the passage says that he shall write a copy of the Torah so "that his heart may not be lifted up above his countrymen" (17:20). In other words, the king must obey the laws of Torah just like everybody else. He has no sovereign exemptions. He has no royal exception or special immunity. By writing a copy of the Torah for himself, the king remembers that he is not above God's law. In the eyes of the Torah, the king is just another citizen of God's kingdom.

THE RULE OF LAW

This basic ethic of Torah is called the Rule of Law. It works similar to the way the constitution of a governing body functions. In theory, a constitution is a document that presides over both the governed and the government. In the constitutional model, ultimate sovereignty is not vested within the government; it lies in the constitution that formed the government.

The Rule of Law is illustrated in the workings of the United States of America. The Constitution of the United States lays out the parameters for American government. Ostensibly, the government can legislate and govern only within those parameters. No government official may overstep the bounds of the Constitution. Government officials are subject to the authority of the Constitution and the legislation spawned by it, just as private citizens are.

Without the Rule of Law, a government would be able to rule capriciously and without mitigation, as is often the case in economies where law has collapsed and violence has prevailed.

In God's economy, the Torah is the constitution that mitigates Israel's government. No one is above God's Torah because no one is above God. His Word is the final authority, and even the king is not to transgress it.

THE SMALLEST LETTER

Knowing all of this, we find it heartwarming to see King Solomon busily engaged in the important commandment of writing a copy of the Torah. But pay attention. Notice the bored and distracted expressions on the faces of the two priests who are supposed to be checking the king's work. Notice the sweat beading up on the king's forehead. Notice his nervous smile as he glances at the priests and then quickly adds a few strokes to the scroll. It looks as if King Solomon has altered the passage he is copying! The priests overseeing the work do not seem to notice.

The king is supposed to be transcribing the words, "He shall not multiply wives for himself, or else his heart will turn away" (Deuteronomy 17:17). But what has the king done? He has erased the little letter *yod* (י) from the word *yirbeh* ("multiply") and replaced it with an *aleph* (א). The *yod* is a letter shaped like an apostrophe and no larger than one, just a small jot of ink. But in replacing that letter with an *alef*, Solomon has changed the whole meaning of the sentence. Now it says, "I will multiply wives and his heart will not turn away." By changing that single letter *yod*, Solomon has changed the meaning. It is a small and subtle change, but now the verse is no longer an imperative forbidding a king to multiply wives. Instead, it states that his multiplication of wives will not have the effect of leading his heart astray. Solomon has removed a jot from the Torah.

AN IMPORTANT MIDRASH

The above scene is more or less described for us in an ancient collection of Jewish teaching called the *Midrash Rabbah*.[115] The passage not only relates this anecdote about Solomon, but also informs our reading of the words of the Master in Matthew 5:

> Do not think that I came to abolish the Torah or the Prophets; I did not come to abolish but to fulfill. For truly I say to you, until heaven and earth pass away, not the smallest letter or stroke shall pass from the Torah until all is accomplished. Whoever then annuls one of the least of these commandments, and teaches others to do the same, shall be called least in the kingdom of heaven; but whoever keeps and teaches them, he shall be called great in the kingdom of heaven. (Matthew 5:17–19)

Some expositors try to make these words say something other than what they say. But the *Midrash Rabbah* and Solomon's unscrupulous scribal editing help us to see clearly the implications of Yeshua's teaching. Let's spend some time analyzing this teaching and its relationship to both Deuteronomy 17 and Matthew 5. The first part of the midrash explains how Solomon reasoned away the literal meaning of the commandment:

> When God gave the Torah to Israel, He gave both positive and negative commands, and He gave some commandments for a king, as it says: "[The King] shall not multiply horses for himself ... He shall not multiply wives for himself or else his heart will turn away ..." But Solomon arose and studied the reason that God gave this commandment, saying: "Why did God command, 'He shall not multiply wives for himself?' Was it not just to keep his heart from turning away? Well, I will multiply wives and my heart will not turn away." (*Exodus Rabbah* 6:1)

In his great wisdom, Solomon supposed he understood the reasoning behind the commandment. Why did the Torah command a king not to multiply wives? Clearly God intended this law as a safeguard for the king's heart. Solomon apprehended the principle of the law. He understood the intention behind the law against multiplying wives. He thus reasoned, "If I keep my heart from going astray, then I am free to multiply wives." Therefore, he felt at liberty to edit the text of the Torah enough to reflect his new insight into God's law.

According to this logic, Solomon could ignore the prohibition on multiplying wives. In his mind, because he understood the principle of the law, he did not need to obey the literal meaning.

To use popular Christian terms, we could say that Solomon did not need to keep the letter of the law because he understood the spirit of the law. If the wise King Solomon had possessed a copy of 2 Corinthians, as we do, he could have quipped, "The letter kills, but the spirit gives life." No more rationalization would have been necessary.

A COMPLAINT IN HEAVEN

The midrash continues with the story of Solomon's edited version of the Torah:

> At that time, the *yod* of the word *yarbeh* went up on high and prostrated itself before God and said, "Master of the Universe! Did you not say that no letter shall ever be abolished from the Torah? Behold, Solomon has now arisen and abolished one. Who knows? Today he has abolished one letter, tomorrow he will abolish another until the whole Torah will be nullified!" God replied, "Solomon and a thousand like him will pass away, but the smallest tittle will not be erased from thee." (*Exodus Rabbah* 6:1)

According to this story, the little letter *yod* that Solomon replaced in his copy of the Torah took such offense that it ascended to God and filed a formal complaint against Solomon. The letter *yod* warned the Almighty that if He allowed this kind of editorial process to continue, the whole Torah would soon be abolished and nullified. God appeased that letter *yod* by assuring it that not even the smallest decorative crown would ever be erased from the eternal Torah. He pointed out that Solomon and men like him are temporal and passing, but the Law of God is eternal. Solomon may ply his wisdom and logic and creative scribal work as much as he likes, but God's Law will still stand long after Solomon has disappeared.

Yeshua seems to have alluded to this story when He forbade His disciples from supposing that He came to abolish the Torah, and reassured them that "not the smallest letter or stroke shall pass from the Torah until all is accomplished."

CLEANING SEWERS

In the midrash, Solomon goes on to explain his rationale. He says, "The reason why God has said, 'He shall not multiply wives for himself' was only lest the king's heart should turn away … God is with me, and I will withstand this temptation."

Solomon felt confident that his own wisdom was superior to the rule of Torah. With a terrific sense of irony the midrash continues:

> Yet what is written of Solomon? "For it came to pass, when Solomon was old, his wives turned his heart away after other gods" (1 Kings 11:4). Rabbi Shimon bar Yochai said, "It would have been better for Solomon to clean sewers than to have this verse written of him." (*Exodus Rabbah* 6:1)

I spent a good number of my younger years engaged in the less-than-glamorous vocation of sewer cleaning. So Shimon bar Yochai's words carry extra color for me. The specific color I am thinking of is the black sludge that invariably accompanies a clogged sewer pipe. It never occurred to me as I labored for hour after hour over clogged sinks, tubs, and toilets that I was better off than Solomon, but the midrash assures me that I was.

In his wisdom, Solomon outsmarted himself. He assumed that because of his rational apprehension of Torah, he rose above the Rule of Law. The thinking goes something like this: "I understand what the Torah really meant by such-and-such a commandment; therefore, I don't need to actually keep that commandment."

I have often heard pastors explain that the laws of clean and unclean animals that forbade Israel from ingesting pork were necessary only because of the absence of refrigeration in the wilderness. Having therefore determined the Torah's reasoning behind the commandment, they claim that we are clearly liberated from keeping this commandment in an age of refrigeration and preservatives.

Likewise, we might be tempted to explain the law of the Sabbath as God's desire for man to take a break from a heavy work week. Understanding the Torah's intention behind the law of the Sabbath, it becomes clear that we need not keep the Sabbath on the seventh day, as long as we take at least one day off every week. Furthermore, since the Torah only intended that we get the rest we need, if we are not tired, we do not need to rest.

We also find it convenient to spiritualize the commandments. The reasoning might go like this: "I understand the meaning of the Sabbath. It teaches us about the Sabbath rest in Messiah. I have no need to literally keep the Sabbath because I understand that the Torah's purpose was only to teach me about the Sabbath rest in Messiah." When we talk like this, it indicates that we have taken our cues from Solomon.

I could go on with more examples of this kind of rationalization. We are all familiar with the ingenious arguments we have constructed to exempt ourselves from the Rule of Law. Somehow, even people who identify themselves as Torah-observant seem to find adequate immunity from the Rule of Law when necessary.

MADNESS AND FOLLY

Regarding Solomon and the unfortunate outcome of his decision to abolish a letter from the Torah, the midrash continues:

> For this reason did Solomon say of himself, "I turned to consider wisdom, madness and folly" (Ecclesiastes 2:12). What Solomon meant by these words was this: He said, "Because I tried to be wiser than the Torah and persuaded myself that I knew the intention of the Torah, my understanding and knowledge turned out to be madness and folly." (*Exodus Rabbah* 6:1)

Solomon's great wisdom turned out to be madness and folly because he thought he was wiser than the Torah. His reinterpretation of the Torah gave him permission to ignore the Rule of Law. He considered himself above the literal meaning of the commandment because he understood the text at a "deeper" level. In so doing, his wisdom turned to madness and folly with bitter consequences in his life.

Are believers in Yeshua exempt from the Rule of Law?

It is true that disciples of Yeshua do not keep the Torah as a means of attaining salvation or access to the family of God. Paul teaches us that salvation is not contingent upon any particular commandment or legal formula but rather upon a gift of grace. God imputes the righteousness of Messiah to us; we do not create it ourselves. There is no magical commandment that when properly observed will suddenly and mystically whisk us from the kingdom of darkness into the kingdom of light.

But it would be madness and folly to assume that we are exempt from the Rule of Law, as Solomon did. We should not assume that, by merit of our salvation, we possess some special immunity to God's commands. It would be madness and folly to cavalierly reinterpret the commandments in such a way as to justify our own disobedience.

THE COST OF DISCIPLESHIP

Yeshua anticipated our tendency to absolve ourselves from the Rule of Law. That is why He reminded us of Solomon's folly when He said, "Do not think that I came to abolish the Torah ... not the smallest letter or stroke shall pass from the Torah."

Without ever having read the midrashic version of Matthew 5:17–19, Deitrich Bonhoeffer incisively explains Yeshua's words regarding the Rule of Law:

> The law Jesus refers to is the law of the Old Covenant, not a new law, but the same law that He quoted to the rich young man and the lawyer when they wanted to know the revealed will of God. It becomes a new law only because it is Christ who binds His followers to it. For Christians, therefore, the law is not a 'better law' than that of the Pharisees, but one and same; every letter of it, every jot and tittle, must remain in force and be observed until the end of the world. Jesus has in fact nothing to add to the commandments of God, except this, that He keeps them. He fulfills the law, and He tells us so himself, therefore it must be true. He fulfills the law down to the last iota. (*The Cost of Discipleship*)[116]

Unlike most of us, Bonhoeffer refused to trivialize and explain away the words of the Master. He took Yeshua literally. Bonhoeffer did not feel the need to be wiser than Yeshua. He did not try to be smarter than the gospel. He did not substitute rationalization for obedience. Because of that, Bonhoeffer met martyrdom in the death camps of Nazi Germany while most of his seminary colleagues were goose-stepping around with swastikas on their uniforms. Bonhoeffer believed in the Rule of Law, and to him, a theology that did not confess the Rule of Law was a theology of "cheap grace."

THE FUNDAMENTAL ETHIC

The Rule of Law is the most basic and fundamental ethic of the Torah. Without the Rule of Law, the ethics of the Torah are reduced to simply good advice, something akin to the fatherly counsel Polonius gives his son Laertes in Shakespeare's *Hamlet*. Without the Rule of Law, the Ten Commandments become the Ten Suggestions.

Yet somehow, we assume that the Rule of Law in the Torah does not apply to us. In so doing, we place ourselves even above the kings of Israel. More than that, we place ourselves above Messiah, the ultimate King of Israel:

> A disciple is not above his teacher, nor a servant above his master. (Matthew 10:24)

New Testament theology requires that Yeshua lived a perfect and sinless life in accordance with the Torah. If He had at any point transgressed Torah, He would have ceased to be the perfect sinless atonement that was necessary in order to pay for our sins. According to Deuteronomy 17, if Yeshua is a true king of Israel, He must keep the Torah "all the days of his life" and carefully observe "all the words of this Torah" and "not turn aside from the commandment, to the right or the left" (Deuteronomy 17:19–20). Therefore, Yeshua was not above the Rule of Law, even though He was, in respect to His concealed, divine nature, the author of that law.

Perhaps our dismay at Solomon's devious edit to the text is a little hypocritical. Christian theology edits out whole sentences, verses, and chapters of the Torah because we have assumed ourselves to be wiser than the Torah. Has our wisdom turned to madness and folly as Solomon's did? Have we taken our cues from King Solomon rather than from King Yeshua? If that is the case, it would have been better for us to clean sewers than to play at theology.

CHAPTER FIFTEEN

The Difficult Laws of Torah

"Are you suggesting we go back to making animal sacrifices?" you may ask. "What about the laws of clean and unclean, and of stoning adulterers and Sabbath-breakers? Surely you aren't suggesting that, as a part of this restoration, believers should return to these antiquated, harsh, and ritualistic laws, are you?

To answer that question, I would like to tell you about Dr. Laura and the Torah.

DEAR ABBY MEETS ELIJAH

Back in the 1990s, American popular culture heard a new voice defending traditional Torah values and norms. At that time, I was working apartment maintenance and often listened to the radio while painting apartments and snaking out clogged sewer drains. That's when I started listening to Dr. Laura Schlessinger on the radio.

Like the voice of the prophets of old, radio talk-show host Dr. Laura preached a message of repentance across the airwaves. A cross between Dear Abby and Elijah the prophet, she made a living out of dispensing advice from a conservative Torah perspective. Her candor and remorseless rebukes made her undeniably entertaining, but what was really unusual was her championing of biblical, ethical values and norms in modern culture. She was not particularly diplomatic. Her political incorrectness so shocked and appalled the popular culture that protests erupted all over the country when she attempted to capture a television audience. The liberal world accused her of being bigoted and homophobic.

Smear campaigns were launched and the protests availed. Advertisers began to pull their sponsorship from the stations carrying her television show. The outcry against Dr. Laura was so great, and her words about morality and decency so insulting to the status quo that television networks quickly removed her show or assigned it to an early morning time slot.

PUSHING THE HOT BUTTON

Was Dr. Laura really a bigot and a homophobe? Probably not. Like many conservative Christians and traditional Jews, she simply took a hard stand on morality. She was not willing to accept the popular notion of moral ambiguity. She regarded God's law as the arbiter of truth, and that entailed a belief in moral absolutes.

But it was not Dr. Laura's defiance of liberal feminism, nor her opposition to day-care parenting, nor her strong pro-life posture that won her the most-hated-conservative status in American culture. The issue that sank Dr. Laura's ship was her refusal to accept homosexuality as a normal and healthy lifestyle. Standing on the ethical ground of the Torah, Dr. Laura declared homosexual behavior to be "abnormal." She did not exactly say it was wrong. She only said it was abnormal.

Her refusal to acquiesce on this issue cost her credibility in the mainstream media, but it won her the love and affection of politically and socially conservative Christians around the country. The condemnation of the homosexual lifestyle was an issue near and dear to their hearts. Few moral issues incited as much vitriolic vehemence among them. Homosexuality has been a hot button in the church for the past three decades, but despite conservative Christian rhetoric against it, the gay agenda has advanced unabated—even within the seminaries of the church itself. Some denominations now officially sanction homosexuality as a viable lifestyle and even perform gay marriages and ordain openly homosexual clergy. The same thing has happened in liberal forms of Judaism like Reform and Conservative, and according to some whispered rumors, even some Messianic Jewish leaders are leaning toward endorsing homosexuality. In 2015, the United States

Supreme Court ruled in favor of making same-sex *marriage* a constitutional right in all states.

Back in the 1990s, the writing was already on the wall. The relentless advance of the gay agenda created such an atmosphere of panic and homophobia in the church that socially conservative Christians were quick to embrace Dr. Laura as one of their own ... even if she was Jewish. Those same conservative Christians were even pointing to the Torah in order to justify the hard moral line they were drawing. But there was a flaw in this method. According to traditional Christian theology, passages like Leviticus 18:22, which unequivocally forbid homosexual relations, were done away with along with the rest of the laws of the Old Testament.

AN ANONYMOUS LETTER

When the Dr. Laura controversy was at its height, I received the following widely circulated email. It was sent to me by a Jewish believer. He had received it from a Christian who was urging him to abandon Messianic Judaism. To this day, it continues to circulate on the internet in different forms. The original version that I received reads as follows:

> Dear Dr. Laura,
>
> Thank you for doing so much to educate people regarding God's law. When someone tries to defend the homosexual lifestyle, for example, I simply remind him that Leviticus 18:22 clearly states it to be an abomination. End of debate. I do need some advice from you, however, regarding some of the specific laws and how to best follow them.
>
> When I burn a bull on the altar as a sacrifice, I know it creates a pleasing odor for the Lord (Lev. 1:9). The problem is my neighbors. They claim the odor is not pleasing to them. How should I deal with this?
>
> I would like to sell my daughter into slavery, as it suggests in Exodus 21:7. In this day and age, what do you think would be a fair price for her? I also know that I am allowed no contact with a woman while she is in her period of menstrual uncleanliness (Lev. 15:19–24). The

> problem is, how do I tell? I have tried asking, but most women take offense.
>
> Now I have a neighbor who insists on working on the Sabbath. Exodus 35:2 clearly states he should be put to death. Am I morally obligated to kill him myself? Then, Lev. 25:44 states that I may buy slaves from the nations that are around us. A friend of mine claims that this applies to Mexicans but not Canadians. Can you clarify?
>
> A friend of mine also feels that even though eating shellfish is an abomination [Deut. 14:3], it is a lesser abomination than homosexuality. I don't agree. Can you settle this? And Lev. 20:20 states that I may not approach the altar of God if I have a defect in my sight. I have to admit that I wear reading glasses. Does my vision have to be 20/20, or is there some wiggle room here?
>
> I know you have studied these things extensively, so I am confident you can help. Thank you again for reminding us that God's Word is eternal and unchanging.

Despite his misapplications and his tendency to violate context, the author of the email to Dr. Laura does make a good case. How can we derive unchanging ethical and moral absolutes from a document we routinely disregard and declare irrelevant to life in the modern world? How can we claim that God's Word is eternal and unchanging while at the same time teach that it has changed?

ABOMINATIONS

In what is certainly his strongest argument, the author of the email compares eating shellfish to homosexuality. Both are described by Torah as abominable to God. The Torah uses the Hebrew word *to'evah* in both instances. The word describes an object that elicits a reaction of disgust and distaste. The word rarely appears in the first four books of Torah, but it finds several applications in Deuteronomy. The book of Deuteronomy tells us that God is disgusted by idolatry, child sacrifice, divination, sorcery, witchcraft, spell casting, channeling spirits, and consulting the dead. In addition, the Torah says that God is disgusted by sexual immorality in worship, gender cross-dressing, remarriage to a previous spouse who has remarried, and inaccurate weights and measures used to defraud.[117] In other words, God is disgusted by sin. The Bible does not make it clear whether those particular sins disgust Him more than others. It should be enough of a deterrent to know that those things disgust the LORD.

In the church in which I grew up, all of the above abominations would have received a resounding "Amen!" In fact, we would have been quick to add Leviticus 18:22 to the list. Therein God describes homosexuality as an abomination to the LORD. But our "amen" would have gotten stuck in our throats if we were told that eating unclean animals is also an abomination to the LORD. How do we reconcile condemning homosexuality while going out for the Red Lobster's all-the-shrimp-you-can-eat special on Friday night?

THREE TORAHS OR ONE?

Typically we reconcile the problem by dividing the Torah into three domains of legislation. The Torah contains laws pertaining to morality, laws pertaining to civil government, and laws pertaining to ceremony. Based upon these three domains of application, our theologians dice the Torah into moral law, civil law, and ceremonial law. We are then able to proceed by saying that the new covenant makes the ceremonial laws and civil laws obsolete. Only the moral code remains valid through the new dispensation of grace.

This explanation seems to satisfy the objections of the disillusioned radio listener who had it out for Dr. Laura. His questions regarding the shellfish, Sabbath, sacrifices, priesthood, and purity laws can all be dismissed as ceremonial laws long ago shed by the true faith. His questions regarding slavery can be dismissed as civil laws, invalidated by the new covenant. Only the moral code remains in force today, and it, happily, includes the prohibition of homosexuality.

The three-fold explanation has one serious flaw. There are not three Torahs. There is only one Torah. The Torah makes no distinction between different categories of laws. For instance, the command to love your neighbor is found right in the middle of what many categorize as Levitical and ceremonial laws of holiness. If you throw those out, you throw out what Yeshua refers to as one of the two most important commandments.

Several years ago, I was invited to teach about Torah at a local Christian Bible school. During the question-and-answer time, one of the students asked, "How can we know if a particular law is moral, civil, or ceremonial? The Bible does not seem to make any distinction." It was an accurate observation. The distinction between moral, civil, and ceremonial laws is somewhat artificial and at times arbitrary.

At no point does Torah give any indication of a separation between moral and ceremonial law. The ceremonial laws of the prohibition of idolatry and the law of the Sabbath are listed in the same list of ten along with the moral statutes regarding murder and theft. The Torah defines eating unclean animals equally abominable as cross-dressing and necromancy. God has not distinguished between ritual laws and ethical laws, but we have.

And because we have, it is possible for some theologians and seminarians to condone homosexuality even in the clergy of the church. Any Scriptures condemning such behavior can be readily dismissed as antiquated ceremonial laws, not part of the essential morality of the Bible. Following this line of reasoning, nothing can be said to be absolutely wrong or right. Rather, everything is subject to possible reinterpretation and dismissal as part of the obsolete body of ceremonial legislation.

By dividing the Word of God into arbitrary categories, some of which we have declared no longer valid, we have dug our own theological grave and handed the shovel to the opponents of the gospel. Now we can only shout in protest as they scoop the dirt in on us. The Dr. Laura email is a big scoop of dirt for which conservative Christianity has no valid answer.

ETERNAL AND UNCHANGING?

The email parodies our misguided handling of Scripture. The anonymous writer astutely observes that we have a double standard when applying Scripture. We use only those passages of Torah that support our moral predispositions. We regard passages that buttress our predispositions as eternal and unchanging. We disregard as obsolete any commandments within Torah that do not support our ethical and religious preferences.

To be fair, the writer takes some liberties with the Torah. Most of his points are made from misapplication of specific commandments. He achieves the ridiculous by taking a commandment out of its context and placing it in a different context.

How we choose to respond to his arguments will either make or break our case against homosexuality and every other moral absolute we ever hope to derive from Scripture. If we allow him to embarrass us into explaining, "Well, those things are ceremonial and cultural things that have been done away with ..." he will say, "The prohibition against homosexuality is also a ceremonial and cultural issue without relevance in the modern world." We may try to bring in passages from the Pauline Scriptures to counter his argument, but these are ultimately futile because Paul derives the authority of his arguments from Torah. If the Torah foundation is malleable, so are the arguments based upon it.

If, however, we maintain that the Torah is unchanging and immutable, as our Master did, we find ourselves on firmer ground. Let's step in for Dr. Laura and my Jewish friend by answering the questions.

SACRIFICE

The emailer points out his neighbor's objections to the burnt offering in the backyard. I can empathize with his neighbor. The sacrifices described in Leviticus are only permitted within the Temple and must be facilitated by a Levitically pure priesthood.[118] In the absence of an existing Temple, the rites of sacrifice cannot be practiced. That is not the same as saying that those laws are obsolete or done away with or canceled. The New Testament metaphorically refers to Yeshua's suffering and death as a sacrifice for sin, but that's not the same as cancelling the sacrifices. The book of Acts shows us that the believers remained engaged in the Jerusalem Temple system long after the death and resurrection of the Master.[119] Obviously they did not regard Temple worship as obsolete.

Ever since the destruction of the Temple in 70 CE, the sacrifices detailed in the Torah have not been possible and will not be possible until God's Temple in Jerusalem is rebuilt. By transferring those laws from their Temple context to the suburban American backyard, the emailer raises some humorous possibilities, but his argument has no real relevance. The Bible does not command him to make a daily sacrifice in his back yard or anywhere else. It commands the priesthood of Israel to do so in the Holy Temple.

PURITY

The email author speculates about contact with ritual impurity; namely women in menstruation. Like the laws of sacrifice, the purity laws have a relevant context only when there is a functional Temple. The purity laws of clean and unclean are designed to protect the sanctity of the Temple precinct, the officiating priesthood, and the sacrifices. In the absence of the Temple, the purity laws are only vestiges of a different world. That does not mean the purity laws are obsolete or canceled. If the Temple were rebuilt in Jerusalem tomorrow, every worshiper going to that Temple would be bound to observe the laws of clean and unclean.

Women in menstruation are only one source of ritual impurity. The emailer selects that particular topic because it will incite the strongest reaction. By transferring those laws from their Temple context to Western, postmodern culture, the author of the email again paints a comical scenario, but one that has no real bearing on the question of the Torah's relevance.

PRIESTHOOD

The reference to the defect in eyesight is actually from Leviticus 21:18, not 20:20, but our comedian has overtaxed himself with the reference to 20/20 eyesight and mistaken it for a verse and chapter reference. (Subsequent versions and generations of the email have been corrected.) Regardless of the error, the eyesight law relates only to the priesthood of Israel, and it refers to blindness, not astigmatism. It is part of a list of prohibitions that forbid a maimed or disabled priest from facilitating the sacrificial service of the Temple.

Our modern sensitivities and equal-opportunity dogmas are offended by a passage like Leviticus 21:18. Like the sacrifices themselves, the priests handling them needed to be without defect. According to the Torah, a priest with a disqualifying defect still enjoyed employment within the priesthood and had the rights to all venues of the priesthood except the sacred service of the altar.

Still, even if the author of the email had perfect vision and was without any form of physical defect, he would be forbidden to approach the altar unless he is a direct and certifiable son of Aaron—not just Jewish, but also a *kohen* (priest). There is no wiggle room here. But again, those laws are relevant only when there is a Temple or an altar to approach in the first place.

SLAVERY

The author of the email plays on emotions evoked by our historical memory of American slavery. He claims that Exodus 21:7 suggests a man sell his daughter as a slave. Actually, the passage in question does not suggest this. Rather, it addresses one of the unpleasant possibilities of life in the ancient Near East where a debtor might find himself or family members forcibly taken into slavery in lieu of unpaid debt. The Torah seeks to protect a woman who might be caught in that barbarous system of economics by ensuring her right of redemption and forbidding her resale to another. Thus, she cannot be used as a sexual slave, passed from owner to owner. She must be treated with dignity and accorded her rights.

The law he criticizes was actually intended to defend the cause of the slave and the rights of women. Far from being obsolete, laws like this one teach the world to treat women—and all human beings—with respect and dignity.

He cites Leviticus 25:44 as granting him permission to buy slaves from Mexico or Canada. This time he is correct. The passage he cites prohibits purchasing Jews as permanent slaves. The Torah allows fellow Israelites to be purchased only on a temporary basis, and then only as a type of hired hand. After seven years, or at the year of Jubilee, the Jewish slave must be released and must be paid for his labor. The same passage does, however, allow for the purchase of Gentiles as lifelong slaves. Other laws in the Torah absolutely forbid kidnapping, so he would need to purchase his slaves from a legal market. Of course, slavery is illegal in Canada, the United States, and Mexico, so even if he were to find some heathens for sale in either Canada or Mexico, he would have other legal issues to deal with. He again makes a satirical point by transferring the world of the ancient Near East into Western society. But pointing out that the Torah legislates against permanently subjugating God's people as slaves is not the same as proving that Torah is no longer relevant.

CAPITAL PUNISHMENT

The author of the witty email accuses his neighbor of Sabbath violations and wonders about the death penalty associated with the sin. The death penalty assigned to Sabbath-breakers and to other grievous sins of Torah was not a vigilante-style execution as our anonymous author imagines. Those sentences were determined through a Torah court of law (namely, the Sanhedrin) employing the adversarial system of justice. The jurisdiction of that court applied only within the land of Israel, and there has not been such a court for nearly two thousand years.

If such a court existed today and had civil jurisdiction in Israel, and if the accused Sabbath-breaker was not a Gentile, but was demonstrably obligated by Torah to keep the Sabbath as Jew, then he would be well-advised to get a good lawyer. The anonymous author of our email could stand as a witness for the prosecution in the trial, but a guilty verdict would not be achievable without an additional witness. Also, intention to belligerently break the Sabbath would have to be proven. If all those criteria were met, then an execution under the auspices of the court could commence.

Maybe it still strikes us as barbaric and antiquated to imagine someone being stoned to death for breaking a ceremonial law such as the Sabbath. Might our self-righteous indignation actually be the result of holding the Sabbath in much lower esteem than God does? We have considerably less trouble imagining a court of law putting a murderer to death because that problem remains a reality in our cultural milieu. The Sabbath is the most often-repeated positive commandment in the Scripture. It may not seem like a big deal to us, but apparently it is to God.

UNCLEAN ANIMALS

The email author drives his finest point regarding the eating of unclean animals. Deuteronomy describes it as an abomination to God, just like homosexuality. Yet even the most right-wing socially conservative Christians enjoy a little lobster tail once in a while. So how can they condemn homosexuality?

Must we acquiesce to the notion that parts of the Torah have been abolished? Or is it possible that we have been wrong about the New Testament cancelling the Bible's dietary laws?

Certainly we could point to several New Testament passages that Christianity has traditionally interpreted as abrogations of the dietary laws, but that would only prove his point about the eternal, unchanging quality of God's Word. If what was called an abomination in one case is now called breakfast, why shouldn't an abomination in another case now be called healthy human sexuality?[120]

THE DIFFICULT LAWS OF TORAH

The Torah contains a plethora of laws that are foreign to us. The laws of the Temple, the sacrificial system, and the purity codes are all outside our world of experience. They were only relevant to worshipers entering the Temple in Jerusalem. The laws of punishments and court-imposed sentences seem, at times, unduly harsh because we have grown accustomed to milder systems of justice—as have society's criminals. But it is important that we do not make arbitrary distinctions, slicing and dicing God's Word in order to make it fit our worldview.

We don't make sacrifices today, but only because the Torah forbids us from doing so. Without a Temple and priesthood, sacrificing is a sin.[121] We don't stone Sabbath-breakers today. The Sabbath's prohibitions do not apply to non-Jews, and to punish a Jew for breaking the Sabbath without first proving before the Sanhedrin that he did so intentionally, flagrantly, knowingly, and deliberately (an impossibility in today's world where the Sabbath is no longer understood or practiced by most Jews) would violate the Torah's own justice system.

When we encounter difficult laws in the Torah, rather than toss them out, we should take the time to study them. That might require some homework on our part. There is only one Torah and every commandment of Torah is a matter of morality, but not every commandment applies in every circumstance or is incumbent upon every individual equally. Some commandments apply only in the land of Israel; some apply only in the Temple or when there is a Temple and priesthood. Some laws apply only to priests. Some apply only to men. Some apply only to women. Some apply only to officers of a Torah court of law. Certain laws are not incumbent upon Gentiles in the same manner that they are upon Jewish people. When studying the Torah, one must consider the context and correct application of the commandments.

In addition, we need to consider how Jewish tradition interprets a commandment. The Jewish community has more than three thousand years of experience in handling the Torah and applying its laws. Oftentimes the rabbis see far deeper into the text than our cursory readings of English translations allow. They bring a wealth of oral tradition and family history to help clarify difficult passages. Before we go any further, we should take some time out from this discussion to consider the role of Jewish tradition in understanding Torah.

CHAPTER SIXTEEN

The Oral Torah

The restoration of the Torah comes with a caveat. We cannot forget that the Torah belongs to the nation of Israel. It comes to us through the Jewish people. Sometimes disciples of Yeshua—both Jewish and Gentile disciples—are eager to take hold of the Torah, but they are reluctant to acknowledge the role of Jewish tradition and authority in interpreting the Torah. We would prefer to interpret the Torah's meaning ourselves and not bother with consulting Judaism, but that's not how the Torah works.

The Apostle Paul says that the "giving of the Torah" belongs to the Jewish people (Romans 9:4). That's a way of saying that the Torah belongs to the Jewish people. When God entrusted the Jewish people with the Torah, He also entrusted them with the responsibility of interpreting its commandments and applying them. He appointed Israel as custodians over the Torah. Judaism calls that custody and stewardship over the Torah by the name "Oral Torah."

To keep things simple, we have been using the words Torah to mean the five books of Moses: Genesis, Exodus, Leviticus, Numbers, and Deuteronomy. Traditional Judaism sees the five books of Moses as only half of the Torah, that is, the Written Torah. In addition to the Written Torah, Judaism teaches the authority of the Oral Torah, the other half of the Torah. The Oral Torah clarifies and interprets the Written Torah.

WRITTEN TORAH: Genesis, Exodus, Leviticus, Numbers, and Deuteronomy

ORAL TORAH: Jewish legal tradition interpreting the laws of the Written Torah.

FROM TRADITION TO MISHNAH

Judaism embedded the specific application of most of the Torah's commandments in its tradition. For example, the Torah requires the Jewish people to set aside the seventh day of the week as holy, but it does not offer a means of reckoning which day the seventh is. Without the continuity of Jewish tradition preserving the reckoning of the week, the commandment could not be practiced with any certainty. Likewise, the people of Israel preserved and transmitted the context and application of many laws that would otherwise remain obscure. The Written Torah often assumes the broader knowledge base and practice of the Jewish people.

In addition, the Torah made the sages, elders, and priesthood responsible for interpreting and applying its laws.[122] Our Master Yeshua affirmed the authority of their interpretations and rulings.[123] The legislators' decisions formed a body of unwritten case precedents. Their disciples transmitted this body of legal lore to subsequent generations. The combination of national practices and the legal rulings form the vast body of Jewish law now called the Oral Torah.

In the days of the apostles, Judaism had not yet developed the term "Oral Torah." The apostolic writers used broader, earlier language to describe the vast body of traditional law and legal interpretations handed down from previous generations: "traditions of the elders," "traditions of the fathers," or simply, "traditions;" "custom of the Jews," "custom of the law," "the customs which Moses handed down," "the customs of our fathers," and "the customs."[124]

The rabbis teach that God originally gave this additional legislation to Moses, who in turn "transmitted it to Joshua, Joshua to the elders, the elders to the prophets, and the prophets transmitted it to the men of the great assembly" in the days of Ezra and Nehemiah.[125] The men of the great assembly passed the tradition on to the rabbis and their disciples.

In the early second century, the famous Rabbi Meir began the dizzying task of committing the gigantic body of oral tradition to writing. A wealthy and prominent distant relative of Yeshua named Rabbi Judah the Prince continued the work and completed what Meir had begun. He created a momentous, skeleton-like, written version of traditional legal material called the Mishnah. The word *mishnah* means "repetition" because, prior to being committed to writing, the material had been passed from generation to generation through memorization via repetition. Rabbi Judah completed the work around 200 CE, and it immediately became the textbook of Torah study for world Jewry.

During the days of the Master, however, the Oral Law remained oral. In those days before codification, competing traditions were, indeed, just traditions, variously practiced, accepted, and argued. In fact, for most people, even the Written Torah was oral. They did not possess a copy of a Bible. They memorized text, and there was not a clear distinction in most people's minds between Oral Torah and Written Torah.

NINE HUNDRED YEARS OF BIBLE STUDY

The Mishnah contains explanations of and expansions on the Written Torah's laws. The need for such explanations and expansions is self-evident. The Written Torah contains numerous commandments that require more information if they are to be observed. For example, the Torah commands Israel to write the Word of God on the doorframes of their houses and on their gates, but it omits the details of how to accomplish this. What passages of the Scripture are to be written? How are the words to be written on the doorframes?

These types of details are elements that the Written Torah assumes its readership already knows or understands. But that assumption breaks down after thousands of years of separation from the original context. The Oral Torah endeavored to preserve those original traditions and pass them on along with the Written Torah.

Many commandments require additional information and details. The great medieval Jewish commentator Maimonides points out that while Israel is commanded to build booths and live in them, no instructions are given regarding the specifics of how to build such a booth. In his introduction to the Talmud, he writes, "Just as we see that the general principles of a commandment were told together with their details and specifics at Sinai, so too, the general principles, details and specifics of all the commandments were told on Sinai." Traditional Judaism holds that Moses wrote down the commandments, but passed on the explanations of the commandments orally:

> It should be understood that every commandment that the Holy One, blessed be He, gave to Moses our Teacher, peace unto him, was given to him together with its explanation. God would tell him the commandment, and afterwards He would give its explanation, its substance, and all the wisdom contained within the Torah's verses. (Maimonides' *Mishneh Torah* quoting *Sifra Leviticus* 25:1)

Judaism, therefore, holds that the Oral Torah carries almost the same authority that the Written Torah carries.

The sages who lived after the compilation of the Mishnah accepted it as the new standard definition of Torah Judaism. In their various schools and academies in Babylon and Israel, they set to work studying and arguing over the Mishnah. Various rabbis told and retold the oral traditions that they had received from their masters. Those traditions sometimes contradicted the Mishnah, resulting in more arguments to try to reconcile with the Torah. In the process, the rabbis traded in old parables, amusing anecdotes, pieces of antiquated laws, rabbinic proverbs, customs, folklore, and superstition. Their conversations and arguments were written down as commentary on the Mishnah called *Gemara,* which means "completion." The Gemara completes the Mishnah because it adds the oral traditions and proof texts and arguments that the Mishnah omitted. In that sense, it completes the Mishnah.

Two prominent schools of sages, one in Israel and one in Babylon, independently produced written Gemara on the Mishnah. The academies in Israel compiled their Gemara on the Mishnah in the fourth and fifth centuries CE, generating a collection called the *Talmud Yerushalami*, i.e., the Jerusalem Talmud. The Babylonian academies compiled their Gemara on the Mishnah to form the even more copious collection called the *Talmud Bavli*, i.e., the Babylonian Talmud. The word *Talmud* means "study." The Talmud, in both versions, is the culmination of nine hundred consecutive years of Bible study—from the first sages quoted in the Mishnah to the last rabbis quoted in Gemara.

MISHNAH: Collection of oral tradition constituting the Oral Torah.

GEMARA: Rabbinic commentary and discussion on the Mishnah.

TALMUD: Compilation of Mishnah with Gemara.

THE BIBLICAL BASIS

Judaism has a biblical basis for the legislation transmitted in the Oral Torah. Deuteronomy 17:8–13 grants Israel's judges and teachers the authority to make legal rulings and instructional interpretations based upon the laws of the Written Torah. Their rulings clarify and apply the Torah. In this way, the Written Torah grants the community leaders in each generation the power to make authoritative and binding decisions for how the Torah is to be lived out and practiced. These rulings are also considered Oral Torah.

Admittedly, the concept of an oral tradition as old as Moses does seem to make sense. Much of the Oral Torah is ancient and some of the contextual implications it provides could well go back to the generation of Moses. The majority of the teachings of the Oral Torah, however, are inferences and extrapolations created by the sages and the rabbis in their attempts to clarify and explain the Torah.

Before we completely throw out the Oral Torah and all its traditions of men, we need to point out that Yeshua retained the authority of Jewish tradition and legislation. He lived in a Jewish world. He engaged in practices derived from both the Written Torah and the Oral Torah. He did this deliberately and with intention. For example, before eating, He always blessed God. The Written Torah commands us to bless God after we eat.[126] Only in the Oral Torah do we learn to bless God before we eat. At His last Passover Seder, He poured wine and shared it with His disciples, even investing significant Messianic symbolism into that Passover cup. The Written Torah, however, says nothing about wine at Passover. Only the Oral Torah mentions the tradition of serving cups of wine as one of the elements of the Passover Seder meal.

Numerous other examples could be cited, but a careful reading of the Gospels makes it clear—Yeshua kept and endorsed traditional Jewish law. This is obvious from the things He did, the things His disciples did, and the traditions the early believers kept. Yeshua firmly endorsed traditional Jewish authority when He told His disciples "The scribes and the Pharisees have seated themselves in the chair of Moses; therefore all that they tell you, do and observe" (Matthew 23:2–3).

YESHUA ARGUES WITH THE PHARISEES

If Yeshua told His disciples to obey the Pharisees and Jewish tradition, why was He always arguing with the Pharisees?

When reading the Gospels, we need to remember that, in the days of Yeshua, the Oral Torah had not yet been codified. Nearly two centuries lie between Yeshua and Rabbi Judah the Prince who compiled the Mishnah. Five centuries stretch between Yeshua and the completion of the Talmud. In the days of the Master, the Oral Torah was still emerging. Importing that fully developed Oral Torah into the first century creates an anachronism. This explains why we see Yeshua arguing the specifics of how to apply Torah much as the sages of the Mishnah and the Talmud argued with one another. In a typical Talmudic argument, Rabbi So-and-So forbids something, but Rabbi Such-and-Such permits it. These arguments constitute most of the Oral Torah. Yeshua was a part of that context, arguing with the sages just like the famous Hillel argued with Shammai.

Gospel readers sometimes assume that Yeshua's arguments with the Pharisees indicate that He rejected Jewish tradition. Yeshua did argue with the religious leaders of His day, but His arguments were about the order of priority, not about the legitimacy of Jewish tradition. He warned people about swallowing camels while straining out gnats. Both are unclean, neither one is kosher, but concern about straining gnats out of the soup should not so preoccupy a person that he fails to notice the soup is actually camel soup.

For example, the Pharisees kept the Jewish tradition of tithing mint, dill, and cumin—items not mentioned in the Written Torah's laws of tithing. Yeshua praised the Pharisees for being so scrupulous and observing the tradition, but He chastised them for doing so at the expense of the weightier matters of the Torah—justice, mercy, and faithfulness:

> Woe to you, scribes and Pharisees, hypocrites! For you tithe the mint and dill and cummin, and have neglected the weightier provisions of the law: justice and mercy and faithfulness; but these are the things you should have done without neglecting the others. You blind guides, who strain out a gnat and swallow a camel! (Matthew 23:23–24)

Almost all of Yeshua's arguments with the religious authorities involve a question of misplaced priorities. For example, first-century Judaism had an obsession with ritual purity. Yeshua argued that purity of the heart, i.e., moral purity, should be a higher priority. Yeshua told the Pharisees, "The things that proceed out of the mouth come from the heart, and those defile the man. For out of the heart come evil thoughts, murders, adulteries, fornications, thefts, false witness, slanders. These are the things which defile the man" (Matthew 15:18–20).

Yeshua argued that compassion for human beings and concerns for human dignity should take precedence over ceremonial concerns. When He went to heal a blind man, He spit in the dirt and mixed the spittle with the dirt to make mud, even though it was the Sabbath. He used the mud to heal the man on the Sabbath. When He healed the cripple, He told him to pick up his mat and carry it. All of those acts—even the very act of healing on the Sabbath day—violated ceremonial prohibitions for the sake of prioritizing compassion for human beings.

EATING BREAD WITH UNWASHED HANDS

In Mark 7, a delegation of Pharisees found Yeshua and His disciples enjoying lunch. The disciples were breaking bread and eating. The Pharisees observed that the disciples had not performed a ritual hand-washing before eating.[127] Once again, Yeshua objected to the Pharisees prioritizing a ceremonial tradition over and above human dignity—this time the dignity of His own disciples.

The Torah requires priests to ritually wash their hands before handling or eating the sacred foods, such as bread made from sacred gifts of first fruits. Some Pharisees had a tradition that applied that same standard to everyone. According to their tradition, every Jew (or at the least, every Pharisee) should wash his hands, like the priests, in order to eat his bread in a state of ritual purity.

The reasoning behind the tradition of ritual hand-washing before eating can be derived from the Torah. In the Torah, human beings can become unclean and even ritually contaminating. For example, someone who has touched a corpse becomes unclean and anyone he touches thereafter will also be rendered unclean.[128] In Leviticus 11:32–38 and Numbers 19 the Torah tells us that otherwise clean food can be rendered unclean when contaminated by ritual defilement.

The Pharisees took these basic biblical concepts and combined them for what would seem to be a logical conclusion. Touching bread with unclean hands renders the bread unclean.[129] According to that interpretation, an unclean person handling otherwise clean food renders that food unclean and thereby unfit for consumption. Thus, if you were unclean (for whatever reason) and went to eat a peanut-butter sandwich with unclean hands, that sandwich would be rendered unclean by your touch. The Pharisees regarded that peanut-butter sandwich as unfit for consumption. One opinion in the Talmud says, "Whoever eats bread without first washing his hands is as though he eats unclean food; as it is written, 'In this way the people of Israel will eat defiled food.'"[130]

If that quotation represents something similar to the conviction of the Pharisees in Yeshua's day, we can understand their shock and disappointment that Yeshua's disciples did not wash their hands according to the traditions of the elders. They could only regard such an abrogation of the religious norm as a strike against His legitimacy. Clearly the man's disciples were not of a Pharisee-caliber.

But does the Torah really require bread to be ritually clean? No, it does not. Not unless it is part of the Temple services or served as a sacred gift to the priesthood.

So they asked Yeshua, "Why don't your disciples walk according to the tradition of the elders?" The Hebrew word *halachah*, "legal application," literally means "the walk." Halachah refers to the specific laws that instruct a person on how to practically walk out the commandments. An argument over how one is to obey a certain commandment or tradition can be called a halachic argument. The Oral Torah determines the halachah.

HALACHAH: Legal rules and applications for practicing the commandments.

The Pharisees were concerned that Yeshua's disciples did not follow the halachah according to the tradition of the elders; namely, washing their hands before eating so that the bread was not rendered unclean by touch. Yeshua defended His disciples by engaging in a sort of halachic argument, the likes of which constitute the seemingly endless pages of the Talmud. He replied with a quote from Isaiah by which He suggested that the Pharisaic requirement of eating bread in a state of ritual purity was a misplaced priority:

> Rightly did Isaiah prophesy of you hypocrites, as it is written: "This people honors Me with their lips, but their heart is far away from Me. But in vain do they worship Me, teaching as doctrines the precepts of men." Neglecting the commandment of God, you hold to the tradition of men. (Mark 7:6–8)

The Pharisaic scruples over hand-washing before eating were not commandments of the Torah; they were only a traditional application. Yeshua knew that obsession with ceremony can serve as a substitute for genuine faith and obedience. He scolded the Pharisees for pursuing ritual purity instead of moral purity. He told them they had set aside the commandments of Torah in favor of their own traditions—specifically, they set aside the prohibition on shaming another person for the sake of their tradition concerning hand-washing.

Jewish tradition and Jewish thought are a rich part of the Torah heritage, but they are not a disciple's source of identity, nor are they a substitute for obedience to the Word. The disciple of Yeshua must always be careful to keep his priorities straight and place the weighty matters of the Torah first.

WHY JEWISH TRADITION?

As explained above, God gave the Torah into the hands of Israel. The Jewish people are the wardens of the Torah, and the Oral Torah represents that stewardship.

Like the Torah itself, Oral Torah applies differently to Jews and Gentiles. Jewish believers should consult Jewish law for determining halachah. That's what it's there for. It's supposed to help you walk out the Torah.

For the most part, the Oral Torah has little to say to Gentile believers. It provides a few broad outlines for Gentiles, but its legislation primarily concerns itself with the application of Torah for Jewish believers. Even so, Gentile disciples will find the oral tradition to be a source of wisdom, godliness, and practical instruction on all matters of Torah.

Some commandments are difficult to obey or understand without the help of tradition. Others are impossible without the clarification tradition provides. Without a common authoritative tradition, we would have no forum for unity. It would be every man for himself. For example, imagine the situation that would ensue if everyone thought they were personally responsible for determining the annual calendar. Everyone would end up celebrating the holy days on different days. The same mayhem would apply to every commandment. Everyone would be responsible for making up his or her own personal religion.

MISAPPLIED TRADITIONS

At the same time, a person should be careful with Jewish tradition. It's easy to misapply it and misinterpret it. For example, Yeshua asked the Pharisees, "Why do you break the commandments of God for the sake of your tradition?" (Mark 7:8). The guiding principle we learn here is that the Written Torah (the Word of God) should always take priority over rabbinic tradition. If a certain custom ever contradicted the Torah, we would need to discard it.

For example, the tradition of lighting Sabbath candles before dark on Friday nights does not contradict the commandment of God. Instead, it helps us honor the Sabbath, sanctify the Sabbath, and keep the Sabbath holy. By requiring Jews to light Sabbath candles before the Sabbath begins, the Oral Torah protects the Jewish people from violating the biblical prohibition against lighting a flame on the Sabbath.[131] So we see that the tradition has a solid biblical footing. If a person finds candle-lighting to be a meaningful part of welcoming the Sabbath, he or she can do so in full confidence. The steady flame of the Sabbath candles can bring warmth to homes and hearts as we celebrate the Sabbath in honor of the Light of the World.

On the other hand, the tradition of lighting Sabbath candles sometimes becomes an end in itself. I have often seen Sabbath candles lit well after the Sabbath has begun on Friday night. When that happens, the commandment of God (not to light a fire on the Sabbath) is set aside for the sake of tradition (lighting Sabbath candles). The tradition, originally meant to protect us from lighting a flame on the Sabbath day, has been misapplied.

DON'T PANIC

Does this mean that to observe the Torah you need to study the Mishnah and the Talmud and halachic discourses? Not at all. That's a job for a rabbi. It's not your job to know all of that. If that was necessary, most people would feel crushed under the sheer weight of the literature. The Mishnah is as dense as a forest. The Talmud is as vast as the sea. Halachic codes of law are tedious and hopelessly obscure to the uninitiated.

This can be compared to civil law. To get around in society without going to jail, you need to know a few basics about civil law, what's legal and what's not legal, but no one expects you to be a lawyer. There might be times in your life when you do need to know some matter of law in greater detail, but when that happens, you hire a lawyer. That's what lawyers are for. Rabbis are, more or less, religious lawyers (among other things).

You don't need to be a Torah scholar to observe the Torah. If you do have questions about specifics, consult your local Messianic Jewish rabbi, or if that's not an option, you might want to consult a few basic books about Judaism. Just make sure they come from reliable sources such as First Fruits of Zion or other Jewish publishers with a traditional perspective. For the most part, that should not be necessary, but it's nice to know where you can get your questions answered when you have them.

A person should not let the weight of Jewish law and Oral Torah discourage him from taking the first steps in Torah observance. For example, suppose you wanted to start keeping the Sabbath. If you waited until you understood all the traditional rules and prohibitions, you would never keep the Sabbath. When it comes to keeping Torah, something is always better than nothing. Do the little bit that you do know to do, and the LORD will bless you in that. Never let yourself feel as if your observance is inadequate because it does not meet the standard of Jewish tradition. The LORD receives everyone who sincerely serves Him from a pure heart, regardless of conformance to traditional standards.

As we approach Torah and Jewish tradition, remember that the goal of Torah is Messiah and the kingdom. As long as we keep our eyes firmly upon the Living Torah, we will be able to find an appropriate balance between the authority of the Written Torah and the directions of the oral tradition. We need look no further than Yeshua. As disciples of the Master, we are imitators of Yeshua. He is our Torah, and His ways are our halachah. It is enough for the student to be like his teacher.

CHAPTER SEVENTEEN

Paul and Torah

Several years ago, I was lecturing at a local evangelical seminary when the dean of the school sensed something amiss with my teaching. He requested a meeting with me. In the privacy of his office, the dean asked about my view of the Law. He was perplexed by my belief that the commandments of Torah are relevant to Christians. I was not explicitly teaching this view in the seminary classes, but word got around.

I explained my position on the matter. I explained that in the Bible, Yeshua and His followers were all Torah-observant Jews practicing first-century Judaism. They kept the Sabbath. They kept the festivals. They kept the dietary laws. I told him that, as an aspiring disciple of Yeshua, I felt that it made sense for me to do the same.

He listened carefully and politely. When I finished, he explained his position on the matter. "You are right," he conceded, "that James the brother of Jesus and the twelve disciples were Jews who continued to practice Judaism. But that is because they did not understand what Jesus was trying to do. That's why the Holy Spirit had to raise up Paul to take the Christian faith out from under the law. The Jewish Christians in Jerusalem misunderstood. They missed the movement of the Spirit."

Those words astonished me. I asked, "So you are suggesting that Jesus' brothers and His disciples didn't get it? They missed the boat?"

He affirmed that this was his belief. In other words, Jesus' efforts on the Twelve were largely wasted. After three years of teaching them and leading them, they still did not understand grace. They had misunderstood what God was doing. Even the brother of Jesus had missed the point. God had to raise up Paul to remedy the disciples' sad devotion to their ancient religion.

I disagreed.

But what about Paul? Didn't Saul the Pharisee convert to Christianity, change his name to Paul, forsake the Torah, and teach freedom from the law? No. He did not.

It is time to take a good, hard look at the Apostle Paul and his relationship to Judaism.

THE PAUL OF ACTS

When we first meet Paul in the book of Acts, we meet a Pharisee and a student of Gamliel, the man who defended the apostles before the Sanhedrin. Paul is a Greek-speaking Jew from Tarsus. His Hebrew name is Sha'ul (Saul); his Greek name is Paul. Contrary to popular Christian legend, Jesus did not change his name from Saul to Paul. Instead, Diaspora Jews commonly had both a Hebrew name and a Greek name. The same custom is common even today among the Jewish people. When among Greek-speakers he used his Greek name, Paul.

Paul never abandoned the Torah. He remained a Torah-observant Jew until the day he died. His enemies claimed otherwise. False rumors circulated about Paul and his work among the Gentiles.

When Paul came to Jerusalem after many years of spreading the gospel among the Gentiles, he met with James the brother of Yeshua and the other elders of the community—the survivors among the Master's original disciples and His family. James presided over the Jerusalem council of elders. History remembers James as a man so devoutly Torah-observant that he was called "the Righteous" even by non-Messianic Jews. The original disciples of Yeshua and the ultra-observant brother of Yeshua voiced their concerns regarding Paul's ministry to the Gentiles. They had heard the rumors that Paul taught against Torah, but they were not willing to believe the slander.

Nonetheless, the Jerusalem elders expressed their concerns, not because they suspected Paul of actually teaching against Torah but because they wanted to clear his name among the believers:

> And they said to him, "You see, brother, how many thousands there are among the Jews of those who have believed, and they are all zealous for the Torah; and they have been told about you, that you are teaching all the Jews who are among the Gentiles to forsake Moses, telling them not to circumcise their children nor to walk according to the customs. What, then, is to be done? They will certainly hear that you have come." (Acts 21:20–22)

According to James and the elders, three specific allegations had been raised against Paul.

1. He taught Jews to turn away from Moses. (Moses = Torah)
2. He taught Jews not to circumcise their children.
3. He taught Jews not to live according to the customs. (Customs = Oral Torah)

Ironically, most Christian theologians have accepted these false allegations as gospel truth. In their zeal to prove that Paul taught against the Torah, they naturally want to believe that the accusations reflect the actual teachings of Paul. According to Christianity's traditional view of Paul, they are quick to agree, "Of course Paul taught against Torah, against circumcision, and against Jewish customs."

But he did not. His opponents and adversaries misconstrued his message to the Gentile believers as an anti-Torah posture. Paul taught the Gentile believers that they did not need to become Jewish (circumcised) and live as Jews (under the full yoke of Torah and Jewish tradition), but he did not teach that message to Jewish believers. His rule for all the churches was that Jews should remain Jewish and Gentiles should remain Gentile.[132] He taught that the Gentile believers needed to observe the Torah's basic ethics (the laws of Noah) and the apostolic decree, but that if a Gentile did become Jewish (circumcised), "he is under obligation to keep the whole Torah" (Galatians 5:3).

James and the Jerusalem elders had already endorsed Paul's message to the Gentiles. They said, "[We] know that there is nothing to the things which they have been told about you, but that you yourself also walk orderly, keeping the Torah. But concerning the Gentiles who have believed, we wrote, having decided that they should abstain from meat sacrificed to idols and from blood and from what is strangled and from fornication" (Acts 21:24–25).

They rejected the notion that Paul was not Torah-obedient. Had Paul been anything other than a Torah-observant Jew, he should have seized the moment to correct the Jerusalem elders. He did not. Instead, he consented to their plan to demonstrate to all of Jerusalem that he was, indeed, Torah-observant.

WHOSE SIDE ARE WE ON?

Why do so many Christian teachers refuse to accept the testimony of Paul, James, the elders of the Jerusalem assembly, and the book of Acts? Instead we have been taught for centuries that Paul renounced Judaism, taught against Torah, and lived a Torahless life as a Christian. It makes me wonder whose side we are on.

James and the Jerusalem elders were eager to clear Paul's name. They knew that when the other Jewish believers heard that Paul had come to Jerusalem, they would demand a formal inquiry into the allegations that he had renounced Judaism. The council of elders chose to act preemptively by suggesting that Paul join several believing Nazirites in a purification ceremony to fulfill their nazirite vows and underwrite the expenses himself. They felt that such a magnanimous and pious act would disprove the allegations and show everyone that Paul was still a faithful, Torah-observant Jew according to the traditions of Judaism.

Paul had undertaken a nazirite vow years earlier when leaving Corinth.[133] Now that he was in Jerusalem, that vow, or perhaps another he had since taken, needed to be completed. To pay for the expenses of four other Nazirites meant coming up with a lot of money. Completion of the nazirite vow requires multiple sacrifices in the Temple. You can read about the nazirite Temple rituals in Numbers 6.

Rather than protest, Paul consented to the plan. He wanted to demonstrate to the believers in Jerusalem that the rumors were false and that he was walking in obedience to the Torah.

PAUL'S OWN TESTIMONY

Throughout the book of Acts, Paul continues to plead his case, protesting his innocence and insisting that he remained faithful to Torah. To the mob that assaulted him in the Temple he declared, "I am a Jew, born in Tarsus of Cilicia, but brought up in this city, educated under Gamaliel, strictly according to the Torah of our fathers, being zealous for God just as you all are today" (Acts 22:3). When standing before the Sanhedrin he asserted, "I have lived my life with a perfectly good conscience before God up to this day" (Acts 23:1). To the Sanhedrin, such a statement could only mean, "I have walked according to Torah." He went on to tell them, "Brethren, I am a Pharisee, a son of Pharisees" (Acts 23:6). Notice the present tense. He did not say, "I was a Pharisee." He said, "I am a Pharisee."

Before Felix, he testified to "believing everything that is in accordance with the Torah and that is written in the Prophets" (Acts 24:14). Before Festus, Paul protested, "I have committed no offense either against the Torah of the Jews or against the temple" (Acts 25:8). Before Agrippa and Bernice he argued, "All Jews know my manner of life from my youth up ... [until imprisonment] I lived as a Pharisee according to the strictest sect of our religion" (Acts 26:4–5). He went on to say, "I stand to this day testifying both to small and great, stating nothing but what the Prophets and Moses said" (Acts 26:22). Finally, in his appeal to the Jewish leadership of Rome, he said, "Brethren ... I had done nothing against our people or the customs of our fathers" (Acts 28:17). If Paul was faithful to keep even the Oral Torah, the "customs of our fathers," how much more so did he keep the Written Torah?

If we teach that Paul renounced Judaism and the Torah's commandments, we deny the testimony of James, the testimony of the Jerusalem elders, the testimony of Luke (the author of Acts) and the testimony of Paul himself.

IN HIS OWN WORDS

Paul's own words on the subject indicate his high regard for Torah. Consider the following passages pulled from Paul's epistles:

For it is not the hearers of the Torah who are just before God, but the doers of the Torah will be justified. (Romans 2:13)

If the uncircumcised man keeps the requirements of the Torah, will not his uncircumcision be regarded as circumcision? And he who is physically uncircumcised, if he keeps the Torah, will he not judge you who though having the letter of the Torah and circumcision are a transgressor of the Torah? (Romans 2:26–27)

Do we then nullify the Torah through faith? May it never be! On the contrary, we establish the Torah. (Romans 3:31)

So then, the Torah is holy, and the commandment is holy and righteous and good. (Romans 7:12)

For we know that the Torah is spiritual. (Romans 7:14)

For I joyfully concur with the Torah of God in the inner man. (Romans 7:22)

Messiah is the end [i.e., the goal] of the Torah. (Romans 10:4)

What matters is the keeping of the commandments of God. (1 Corinthians 7:19)

Therefore the Torah has become our tutor to lead us to Messiah, so that we may be justified by faith. (Galatians 3:24)

We know that the Torah is good, if one uses it lawfully. (1 Timothy 1:8)

Keep the commandment [i.e., Torah] without stain or reproach. (1 Timothy 6:14)[134]

All Scripture is inspired by God and profitable for teaching, for reproof, for correction, for training in righteousness; so that the man of God may be adequate, equipped for every good work [of Torah].[135] (2 Timothy 3:16–17)

These are not the words of a man who turned his back on God's Torah.

PAUL'S ARGUMENT

Why is it, then, that so many Pauline passages seem to dismiss the Torah and even encourage us not to keep the Torah?

We live in a day when the majority of Christians do not keep the ceremonial aspects of Torah such as Sabbath, festivals, dietary laws, and so forth. In Paul's day, the majority of the disciples of Jesus did. When we read Paul's letters, it sounds to us as if he is defending modern Christianity as we know it, but Paul did not live in our day. He never knew modern Christianity or even the Christianity of the second-century church fathers. In Paul's day, believers were part of the larger Jewish community. They still honored the seventh-day Sabbath as the regular day of worship. They still attended synagogues. They still observed strict dietary laws. In addition, Gentile disciples felt enormous social pressure to become Jewish. Paul's letter must be understood within this larger Jewish context.

Remember that when we read Paul's letters, we hear only one side of an argument. The Apostle Paul found himself repeatedly locking horns with other Jewish believers over the role and position of non-Jews in the kingdom of heaven. His opponents asserted that before a Gentile could be saved, he must become Jewish: "It is necessary to circumcise them and to direct them to observe the Law of Moses" (Acts 15:5). Paul disagreed.

In his epistle to the Galatians, Paul responded to his theological opponents' teaching by warning the Gentile believers in Galatia from becoming circumcised, i.e., from becoming Jewish.[136] He argues strongly against compelling Gentiles to be "under the law" (i.e., to become Jewish) in all of his epistles. In the case of disciples with Jewish heritage, however, Paul did not hesitate to circumcise them as Jews. He personally oversaw Timothy's circumcision. Gentiles like Titus or the Galatian Gentile believers he encouraged to remain uncircumcised.

UNDER THE LAW: Pauline term for becoming legally Jewish

CIRCUMCISED: Pauline term for someone legally Jewish

Paul argued against requiring non-Jewish believers to adopt the particulars of Torah that defined Jewish identity. If Paul ever did command his non-Jewish readers to "remember and observe the Sabbath, keeping it holy," or any other aspect of Torah incumbent only upon Jews, he would have been overturning his own argument. His words would have become ammunition for those in favor of requiring the Gentiles to become Jewish.

When we read Paul outside the context of this argument, we are apt to misunderstand him completely. If we forget that Paul argued against requiring Gentiles to become Jewish, we might suppose that he lodged his arguments against Judaism and the Torah.

PAUL AND THE DISCIPLES OF YESHUA

Yeshua commissioned His disciples to go forth and make disciples of all nations, teaching them to obey everything He had commanded (Matthew 28:19–20). Paul was not one of the twelve disciples who originally heard this commission, but he certainly took up the mantle of discipleship and the commission of apostleship. Any discussion of Paul's attitude toward Torah should factor in his radical discipleship to Yeshua.

The Apostle Paul told the Corinthians, "Be imitators of me, just as I also am of Messiah. Now I praise you because you remember me in everything and hold firmly to the traditions, just as I delivered them to you" (1 Corinthians 11:1–2). In his second letter to the Thessalonians he warned the believers to stay away from those who had abandoned the oral traditions that he had taught and modeled while with them:

> Now we command you, brethren, in the name of our Lord Yeshua the Messiah, that you keep away from every brother who leads an unruly life and not according to the tradition which you received from us. For you yourselves know how you ought to follow our example, because

> we did not act in an undisciplined manner among you. (2 Thessalonians 3:6–7)

Paul taught a life of imitation of Yeshua. Disciples are more than just converts. Disciples must meet expectations of discipleship. "A disciple is not above his teacher; but everyone, after he has been fully trained, will be like his teacher" (Luke 6:40). To be like Yeshua, Paul needed to observe the Torah, and his disciples needed to observe it as it applied to them.

THE MYSTERY OF LAWLESSNESS

Paul is regularly accused of disposing of the Torah. A careful, contextual reading of his writings, however, reveals just the opposite. Paul was a faithful Jew, practicing Judaism along with the rest of the Jewish people. So why is he depicted as a man of lawlessness?

Ironically, Paul actually talks about a "man of lawlessness." He uses that title to describe the Antichrist: the man of Torahlessness:

> [The end] will not come unless the apostasy comes first, and the man of lawlessness is revealed, the son of destruction, who opposes and exalts himself above every so-called god or object of worship, so that he takes his seat in the temple of God, displaying himself as being God. Do you not remember that while I was still with you, I was telling you these things? The mystery of lawlessness is already at work; only he who now restrains will do so until he is taken out of the way. Then that lawless one will be revealed … the one whose coming is in accord with the activity of Satan, with all power and signs and false wonders, and with all the deception of wickedness." (2 Thessalonians 2:3–10)

Far from being a man of lawlessness, Paul warns us against the Man of Torahlessness: the Antichrist. Paul indicates that we will be able to recognize this imposter because he will be opposed to the Torah of God. We can use the Torah as a standard of measurement to distinguish a false prophet from a real prophet and a false messiah from the real Messiah. Paul lamented that even in his own day, Antichrist's spirit of Torahlessness was already at work. If the spirit of lawlessness was already at work in Paul's day, how much more so in our own?

PAUL IN CONTEXT

In order to read Paul in context, we must remember that Paul remained a Torah-observant Jew practicing Judaism his entire life. He wrote to Gentile believers who, for the most part, already congregated in synagogues or house churches on the Sabbath and participated in Jewish life along with the broader Jewish community. They kept the Torah as it applied to them as Gentiles.

We must also remember Paul's argument for the inclusion of the Gentiles. Paul argued against other believers—theological opponents—who resisted the inclusion of Gentile believers. They insisted that Gentiles could not be saved unless they first became Jewish.

When we fail to remember that context, we misunderstand Paul's letters. Even in the first century, one could fairly say that Paul's letters contain "some things hard to understand, which the untaught and unstable distort, as they do also the rest of the Scriptures, to their own destruction" (2 Peter 3:16). If it was easy to misunderstand Paul in those days, how much more so in our own day? For that reason, we should not be surprised when people misunderstand Paul's arguments.

CHAPTER EIGHTEEN

Res-Torah-ation

I believe that God is restoring His people in our day. He has begun by returning the Jewish people to their ancient homeland. At the same time, He is returning His Torah to the disciples of Yeshua.

CONFESSIONS OF A "JUDAIZER"

From my perspective, there is even more at stake than prophetic destiny. I am concerned for the reputation of Yeshua and the integrity of our faith in Him. I love our faith and our Master. I teach and write about the Torah in defense of the legitimacy of our hope in Messiah. I believe that without the restoration of Torah, we risk discrediting Messiah. Let me explain.

Moses warned Israel about false prophets. Most people who claim to be prophets are not. Generally, this is self-evident. A false prophet may predict something that fails to transpire, or he might produce a sign or wonder that fails to signify anything wondrous. According to Moses, such a prophet has "spoken presumptuously" and is to be put to death (Deuteronomy 18:20–22).

Even if the would-be prophet's sign or wonder does succeed and his prediction does come to pass, that does not make him a legitimate prophet. He might still be a false prophet. Signs and wonders do not prove that God has sent him. If the prophet attempts to dissuade Israel "from the way in which the LORD your God commanded you to walk" (Deuteronomy 13:5), the people must disregard him as a false prophet. The "way in which the LORD your God commanded" Israel to walk is the Torah and its commandments. Moses warns us that we must not listen to any prophet who turns Israel away from the Torah, even if his ministry comes with amazing signs and wonders. Instead, the Jewish people are to "follow the LORD … keep His commandments, listen to His voice" (Deuteronomy 13:4).

Jewish law refers to the type of false prophet described in Deuteronomy 13 as "an enticer." An enticer is any miracle-worker who entices the Jewish people to turn from the Torah. If the would-be prophet counsels the Jewish people to break the commandments, he must be deemed a false prophet. For example, an alleged prophet who declared that God had sanctioned an adulterous relationship can be immediately identified as a false prophet because he has contradicted Torah. God does not contradict His own word.

False prophets can perform miracles, signs, and wonders. Moses says that a false prophet might be allowed to perform signs and wonders in order to test Israel's fidelity to Torah. The Master warns us that "false prophets will arise and will show great signs and wonders" (Matthew 24:24).

IS JESUS A FALSE PROPHET?

According to God's own criteria for determining a false prophet, Judaism's rejection of the traditional Christian presentation of Jesus is a matter of obedience to Torah and loyalty to God. The traditional presentation of the Christian Jesus offers a prophet (and much more than a prophet), attested by signs and wonders, who canceled the Torah. Such a person fits the Torah's description of a false prophet perfectly. Conversion to faith in such a person or obedience to such a person would certainly violate God's commandments. The Talmud accuses Yeshua of this crime, of enticing Israel to idolatry, and it cites Deuteronomy 13 as grounds for His execution:[137]

> You shall not yield to him or listen to him; and your eye shall not pity him, nor shall you spare or conceal him. But you shall surely kill him; your hand shall be first against him to put him to death. (Deuteronomy 13:8–9)

The real Yeshua of the Gospels is not such. He has little affinity with the traditional depiction of the Christian Jesus in regard to the Torah and the Jewish people. Our Master Yeshua is a prophet (and much more than a prophet) attested to by signs and miracles, but He taught the enduring, unchanging Torah and called Israel to submit to the highest standards of Torah.

His opponents among the Judean leadership labored hard to find some way of demonstrating that He was a breaker of Torah. If they had been able to prove that He taught against Torah, they could have invalidated His claims. They were unable to do so. Nevertheless, traditional Christian theology has consistently presented Him as a prophet teaching against the Torah. A Messiah that breaks Torah and teaches others to do so is no Messiah at all.

An anecdote from Jewish-Christian dialogue illustrates this point well:

> Christian leaders in Czarist Russia held debates in which they attempted to persuade the Jewish community to accept Jesus for Messiah. At one point, they listed off all the signs, wonders. and miracles which Jesus performed in the Gospels as evidence of Messianic claims. One of the Sages of the Jewish community stood up and asked, "Are not the teachings of the Nazarene based upon the Torah of Moses?" When the Christians conceded that they were, the Sage continued saying, "Our Torah unequivocally and clearly prohibits us from abolishing any commandment of the Torah at the behest of a prophet who performs miracles. It says, 'You shall not listen to the words of that prophet ... for the LORD your God is testing you'" (Deuteronomy 13:3).[138]

Missionaries typically present Yeshua to the Jewish people as a miracle-worker who has thrown off the Torah and invites them to do so as well. They tell the Jewish people, "Become a Christian and you will no longer be under the Law." According to the Bible's own criteria, we thereby disqualify Yeshua as a potential prophet. Such a man is not even a true prophet, much less the Messiah. Our presentation of the Torahless Yeshua is self-defeating and discredits Messiah and His message. We bring shame on the gospel and on the name of Messiah.

If the Word of God is true, it must be consistent. If Messiah is true, He must be consistent with the Torah of Moses. The true Yeshua described in the New Testament is consistent with the Torah, but the traditional Jesus Christ who breaks the Torah and sets us free from the Law is not.

I desire to see the gospel restored. Just as the Jewish people are being restored to the land of Israel, I hope to see the message of the gospel restored. That is why I am passionate about restoring the gospel to its original context. I am not a legalist, nor am I a Judaizer. I am a believer in Yeshua and one of His disciples, and I believe that our faith is worth defending. If we have made mistakes in the past, let's own up to them and move on.

DESTROYED FOR LACK OF KNOWLEDGE

For nearly two thousand years, the Jewish people have languished in exile, without a king, without a Temple, and without a home. How did this happen? According to the Bible, it happened because the Torah was neglected.

The Bible says that neglect of the Torah leads to idolatry, apostasy, and exile. In the days of kings and prophets, neglect of the Torah brought the kingdom of Judah to the brink of disaster, "For they have rejected the Torah of the LORD of hosts and despised the word of the Holy One of Israel" (Isaiah 5:24).

Israel and Judah went into exile for turning away from the Torah. "They have not listened to My words, and as for my Torah, they have rejected it also" (Jeremiah 6:19). "Me they have forsaken and have not kept My Torah" (Jeremiah 16:11). "Nor have they feared nor walked in My Torah or My statutes … Therefore … Behold, I am going to set My face against you for woe, even to cut off all Judah" (Jeremiah 44:10-11). "My people are destroyed for lack of knowledge. Because you have rejected knowledge, I also will reject you … Since you have forgotten the Torah of your God, I also will forget your children" (Hosea 4:6).

The Temple was destroyed because the people transgressed the Torah. "Like an eagle the enemy comes against the house of the LORD, because they have transgressed My covenant and rebelled against My Torah" (Hosea 8:1). "If you will not listen to Me, to walk in My Torah which I have set before you ... then I will make this house like Shiloh, and this city I will make a curse to all the nations of the earth" (Jeremiah 26:4–6).

If turning away from the Torah inflicted the wound, then returning to Torah is the balm.

In a sense, the gospel has been in exile since the days of the apostles. Like the Jewish people sent into exile to wander among the nations, the gospel has been dispersed among the nations and subject to the Gentiles. Like the Jewish people wandering far from home, the gospel has traveled far removed from its Jewish context. Today, the exile is coming to an end.

FOUR THINGS THAT NEED RESTORING

As the exile comes to an end and we prepare for the redemption, we should be working together to restore the Jewishness of Yeshua, restore the authentic message of the gospel, restore the authority of the Torah, and restore Israel's status as the people of God.

We want to restore a clear understanding of Yeshua's relationship with the Jewish people and also His relationship with the land of Israel. Yeshua is Jewish. When He comes again, He will still be Jewish. Yeshua's life was rooted in the land and in the Judaism of His day. Although He is Jewish, His message applies to everyone. He is expanding the commonwealth of Israel by gathering all the nations into the blessing and spiritual family of Abraham (Genesis 12:3).

We want to restore the true good news (gospel) preached by Yeshua: Repent, for the kingdom of heaven is at hand. This true gospel message focuses on the coming kingdom of heaven, and it demands a response in the form of genuine repentance. It entails contrition, the forgiveness of sins, and personal transformation in Yeshua's name. The true good news calls upon everyone to seek first the kingdom: the Messianic Age (Matthew 6:33).

We want to restore the Torah's authority as God's unchanging standard. The Torah is the universal revelation of God's will and wisdom through His people Israel. It contains commandments pertaining to both Jews and Gentiles. The Torah defines sin and points mankind toward righteousness and godliness. Until heaven and earth pass away, not an iota, not a dot, will pass from the Torah until all is accomplished (Matthew 5:18).

We want to restore Israel's status as the people of God among the disciples of Yeshua by eliminating replacement theology and Christian anti-Semitism. The Jewish people are God's people—the chosen people, a holy nation, and a kingdom of priests. From Genesis 12 to Revelation 22, the Jewish people are at the center of the Bible and the center of God's concern. The LORD has not abandoned His people, nor has He exchanged them for another. So long as the sun, the moon, and the stars endure, the people of Israel will never cease from being a nation before the LORD, nor will He cast them off (Jeremiah 31:36-37).

SOME MAY DISAGREE

Not everyone will share my theological convictions. Not everyone who reads this book will come to the same conclusions. But at the least, I hope we can begin to reorient the way we think about Yeshua and His relationship to the Torah and Judaism. We should agree to read the Gospels and the Epistles from a Jewish perspective. We should agree that the true Yeshua of Nazareth is a Jew who lived a pious Jewish life, in full accord with the commandments of God.

Within the Messianic Jewish movement today, a healthy debate continues about how the Torah applies to non-Jewish believers in Yeshua. I believe that the Torah applies to all God's people—not just to the Jewish people, but also to those who have been grafted into the greater commonwealth of Israel and who now live as spiritual sojourners among the people of Israel. Gentile believers are not responsible for every commandment that is incumbent upon a Jewish person, but most of the commandments, particularly the weighty matters of the Torah, apply equally to all believers.

Others may disagree with this position, but I hope we can all agree that God's chosen people Israel have not been replaced, and neither has His Holy Torah been abolished. If we can begin to move past the old theological slogans and recognize that the Jewish people remain God's people and that the Torah is still His law, then we have come a long way already. The nightmares of our history and the atrocities of our historic anti-Semitism can be left in the past. We need not carry them into the future.

THE RESTORATION

In the church today, one often hears the mantra, "God is doing a new thing." This catchphrase is usually offered to explain the latest popular fad or charismatic wave to wash up on the beach of religious expression.

I believe that God is doing an old thing.

God, who never changes, is pouring out the same message He has always delivered through His holy prophets; "Return to My Torah. Obey My commandments." Moses predicted this time of restoration when he said, "And you shall again obey the LORD, and observe all His commandments which I command you today" (Deuteronomy 30:8).

Around the world, spontaneously and simultaneously, disciples of Yeshua are rediscovering the Torah. They are asking questions. They are seeking answers. They are knocking at the ancient gates. For the first time in almost two thousand years, believers are taking on the Master's easy yoke. It is not a matter of legalism or heavy bondage; it is a matter of love:

> He who has My commandments and keeps them is the one who loves Me; and he who loves Me will be loved by My Father, and I will love him and will disclose Myself to him. (John 14:21)

I believe that in these last days, God is preparing a remnant of believers who will walk and live according to His commandments. In the last days a remnant of believers will stand against the mystery of lawlessness. They will "keep the commandments of God and hold to the testimony of Yeshua" (Revelation 12:17). If God is to fulfill this prophecy, He must first raise up a remnant of believers who keep the commandments of God.

Inspired by the Holy Spirit, many disciples of Yeshua, Jewish and Gentile alike, are feeling a deep longing to return to the Torah. The prophets predicted it:

> Now it will come about that in the last days ... many peoples will come and say, "Come, let us go up to the mountain of the LORD, to the house of the God of Jacob; that He may teach us concerning His ways, and that we may walk in His paths." For the Torah will go forth from Zion, and the word of the LORD from Jerusalem. (Isaiah 2:2–3)

As the world gropes in the darkness, men and women from all walks of life are heeding this call of God's Spirit to return to the firm foundation laid in the Word thousands of years ago. Far from being some new, innovative fad, the return to Torah is a restoration of something old.

The LORD has declared, "Stand by the ways and see and ask for the ancient paths, where the good way is, and walk in it; and you will find rest for your souls" (Jeremiah 6:16). The ancient paths are the paths of Torah. The good way is the way of the Master, the way of discipleship. He has declared, "Take My yoke upon you and learn from Me, for I am gentle and humble in heart, and you will find rest for your souls. For My yoke is easy and My burden is light" (Matthew 11:29–30).

APPENDIX

The Apostolic Decree

EXCERPT FROM TORAH CLUB: CHRONICLES OF THE APOSTLES

> The apostles and the brethren who are elders, to the brethren in Antioch and Syria and Cilicia who are from the Gentiles, greetings. Since we have heard that some of our number to whom we gave no instruction have disturbed you with their words, unsettling your souls, it seemed good to us, having become of one mind, to select men to send to you with our beloved Barnabas and Paul, men who have risked their lives for the name of our Lord Jesus Christ. Therefore we have sent Judas and Silas, who themselves will also report the same things by word of mouth.
>
> For it seemed good to the Holy Spirit and to us to lay upon you no greater burden than these essentials: that you abstain from things sacrificed to idols and from blood and from things strangled and from fornication; if you keep yourselves free from such things, you will do well. Farewell. (Acts 15:23–29)

The apostolic decree follows the basic form of a first century epistle, naming first the sender, then the recipient, followed by a salutation and the body of the letter. In this case, the sender is "the apostles and brethren who are elders," that is, the leadership of the Jerusalem community. They address the letter "to the brethren in Antioch and Syria and Cilicia who are from the Gentiles." The apostolic leaders addressed the letter specifically to Syria and Cilicia because the disciples there had raised the question. It does not mean that the ruling applied only in Syria and Cilicia. Paul brought the ruling with him to communities beyond those borders, "delivering the decrees which had been decided upon by the apostles and elders who were in Jerusalem, for them to observe" (Acts 16:4).

The letter opened with a disavowal of the men who had gone to Antioch and raised the issue (Acts 15:1). James and the apostles made it clear that those men did not represent them. Some manuscripts state, "We have heard that some of our number to whom we gave no instruction have disturbed you with their words, unsettling your souls, saying, 'You must be circumcised, and keep the Torah,' to whom we gave no such commandment" (Acts 15:24).

The epistle affirmed Barnabas and Paul as beloved brothers who had risked their lives for the sake of the Master. The letter endorsed their message, and it made mention of Barsabbas and Silas, the messengers entrusted with the decree. Finally, it reported the council's ruling, "For it seemed good to the Holy Spirit and to us to lay upon you no greater burden than these essentials. That you abstain from things sacrificed to idols and from blood and from things strangled and from fornication; if you keep yourselves free from such things, you will do well. Farewell" (Acts 15:28–29). The epistle offered no further explanation of the four prohibitions. It indicated that Silas and Barsabbas would provide further explanation by word of mouth.

The following explanations may help clarify the intention behind each of the four essentials and point out the Torah's corollary obligations.

THINGS CONTAMINATED BY IDOLS

> That you abstain from things sacrificed to idols (Acts 15:29)

The seven universal laws of Noah and the basic, minimum standard of Jewish monotheism forbade the worship of idols. Both the worship and creation of graven images was forbidden. The apostolic decree held Gentile believers to an even higher standard. As strangers dwelling within Israel, God-fearing Gentile believers also had to avoid "things contaminated by idols" (Acts 15:20) and especially "things sacrificed to idols" (Acts 15:29). This required them to utterly renounce idolatry and things associated with *avodah zarah* ("foreign worship").[139]

As noted above, the basis for the prohibition appears in Leviticus 17:7–9, which the Torah applies to both the Jewish people and to the "aliens who sojourn among them." The Torah further develops the prohibition against bringing "an abominable thing into your house" (Deuteronomy 7:26). One must not derive any benefit whatsoever from idols or from anything that has been offered up to an idol. In another pertinent passage, the Torah warns the people not to "whore after their gods," "sacrifice to their gods," or "eat of [a pagan's] sacrifice," that is, food connected to any type of idolatrous ritual.[140]

In the book of Revelation, the resurrected Yeshua condemns those who indulge in foods sacrificed to idols.[141] Early church writers like Justin Martyr, Clement of Alexandria, Irenaeus, Tertullian, and even the fifth-century church father Augustine maintained the prohibition.[142] For example, in his dialogue with Trypho, Justin Martyr says, "Those of the Gentiles who know God, the Maker of all things through Jesus the crucified, patiently endure every torture and cruelty even to the point of death, rather than worship idols or eat meat offered to idols."[143] The *Didache* warns, "Scrupulously guard yourself from what has been offered to idols, because it is the worship of dead gods."[144]

Numerous commandments in the Torah deal exclusively with forbidding idolatry and all forms of *avodah zarah*. The apostolic decree obligated the God-fearing Gentiles to keep those commandments whenever applicable. They wanted the new believers to make a clean break from their idolatrous past and cling to the God of Israel. Therefore, all the Torah's commandments regarding idolatry (except for civil punishments) are binding on Gentile disciples. In summary, the prohibition on things polluted by idols includes most of the Torah's commandments pertaining to idolatry, paganism, and the occult.

BLOOD AND THINGS STRANGLED

> That you abstain ... from blood and from things strangled. (Acts 15:29)

The seven laws of Noah forbade God-fearing Gentiles from eating the flesh of a living creature, but, based on Leviticus 17:10, the apostolic decree held the Gentile believers to a higher standard by forbidding them from consuming blood and the meat of strangled animals.

Many commentators have suggested that the apostolic decree against "blood" is a prohibition on bloodshed. This explanation is problematic because, if so, one would need to explain why the apostles felt it necessary to explicitly forbid murder but said nothing about assault, kidnapping, theft, and so forth. Moreover, as explained above, the laws of Noah already prohibited murder. A decree against bloodshed would be redundant.

The prohibition on blood forbids disciples of Yeshua from consuming blood in any form. Early Christians carefully observed the prohibition on blood. One late second-century Christian boasted, "We do not use even the blood of edible animals in our food."[145] Tertullian (160–220 CE) reports that Christians "do not even allow the blood of animals at their meals of ordinary, natural food." He also reports that, during times of persecution, the Romans tested those suspected of being Christian with blood: "You test Christians with sausages of blood, only because you are perfectly aware that the thing by which you try to get them to transgress they hold unlawful."[146]

The related prohibition on "things strangled" forbids disciples of Yeshua from eating the meat of animals that have not been ritually slaughtered according to the traditional Jewish method. The prohibition on strangled meat is just the "negative corollary" to the positive commandment in Leviticus 17:13 to "pour out the blood."[147] The Mishnah uses the term "strangled" to refer to animals improperly slaughtered.[148] Philo uses the same terminology, as does the apocryphal work *Joseph and Asenath*.[149] When interpreted in the Jewish framework within which the injunction was given, "things strangled" is directly related to the prohibitions against "blood":

> "Strangled meat" referred to animals that had been slaughtered in a manner that left the blood in it. Blood was considered sacred to Jews, and all meat was to be drained of blood before consuming it. The prohibition of "blood" came under the same requirement, referring to the consumption of the blood of animals in any form. These three requirements [abstention from food sacrificed to idols, things strangled, and blood] were thus all ritual, dealing with matters of clean and unclean food.[150]

> "What has been strangled," i.e., meat from animals improperly or not ritually butchered, without having the blood drained from them (Leviticus 17:15, cf. 7:24; Exodus 22:31).[151]

> "'Strangled meat' i.e., meat from animals not slaughtered by pouring out their blood, in conformity with biblical and Jewish practice."[152]

According to Jewish law, the meat of improperly slaughtered animals retains the lifeblood of the animal. The ancient Jewish method of slaughter was derived from the sacrificial procedure of the holy priesthood, and it is meant to remove as much blood as possible.[153]

Most Christians no longer abide by this apostolic rule, but early Christians did. Even after their separation from Judaism, Gentile Christians still observed the apostolic prohibition against consuming blood and meat from non-kosher slaughter. Tertullian says, "[Christians] abstain from things strangled or that die a natural death. They do so only to avoid contracting [ritual] pollution, abstaining even from blood secreted internally."[154] Second-century Gentile believers in France still purchased kosher-slaughtered meat long after the church had begun severing its ties from Judaism.[155] Naturally, the God-fearing Gentile believers also avoided the meat of unclean animals—not as a matter of absolute obligation but because of the Jewish context of their communities. So long as the God-fearing Gentile Christians purchased their meat only from Jewish slaughterers, they avoided unclean mammals such as swine and camel by default. Nevertheless, the apostolic decree does not specifically forbid the meat of unclean animals, but it does forbid the meat of strangled animals. As mentioned earlier, Apostolic-era voices in the *Didache* went further and encouraged Gentiles to voluntarily adopt a more kosher diet:

> If you can bear the whole yoke of the Lord, you will be complete; but if you cannot, then do what you can. Concerning food, bear what you can, but scrupulously guard yourself from what has been offered to idols, because it is the worship of dead gods. (*Didache* 6:2–3)

"Yoke of the Lord" here refers to the Torah. The apostles allowed for those unable to bear that yoke. In any case, at a minimum, Gentile disciples are obligated to keep the Torah's prohibitions on consuming blood and the meat of animals that have not undergone a kosher slaughter.

Ironically, most Gentile believers are unaware of these prohibitions or simply disregard them. As Rabbi Lichtenstein observes, Christians are at a loss to explain why the apostles required these laws:[156]

> This is a difficulty in the minds of the preachers and commentators. They claim that the old Torah was completely annulled along with its ceremonial statutes. Then why did the apostles impose on the Gentiles the prohibition against strangled meat and the prohibition against consuming blood? In reality, the Gentile Christians are not careful to think these matters through.

FORNICATION

> Abstain … from fornication; if you keep yourselves free from such things, you will do well. Farewell. (Acts 15:29)

The seven laws of Noah forbade God-fearing Gentiles from sexual immorality, but in the days of the apostles, the sages left sexual immorality, as it applied to Gentiles, undefined. The apostles held the Gentile believers to a higher standard on the basis of Leviticus 18:26: "You shall not do any of these abominations, neither the native, nor the alien who sojourns among you." Therefore, the apostolic decree forbids the Gentile believers from acts of sexual immorality as defined by Torah law. The Torah offers over twenty-five commandments dealing with proper sexual relations. As noted above, Leviticus 18 forbids bestiality, homosexuality, incest, and sexual relations with a woman during her monthly cycle (*niddah*). Leviticus 15 gives further details regarding this injunction including a minimum length of time for the period of separation.

Based on Leviticus 18:6, which states, "None of you shall approach any one of his close relatives to uncover nakedness," Judaism enforces safeguards that prevent even hints or appearances of sexual immorality. The Hebrew word for "nakedness" (*ervah*) has a wider connotation of immodest behavior in general. The sages reasoned that if one should be careful not to even approach one's "blood relative" (i.e., one's family member with whom sexual relations are unlikely), how much more so with non-relatives. For that reason, non-relatives of opposite gender do not touch. An unmarried man and woman do not seclude themselves or spend time alone. Men and women dress modestly and conduct themselves in such a manner as to guard against even the appearance of evil.[157] Naturally, the laws of sexual propriety and modesty include the prohibition on cross-dressing.[158] All these issues fall under the general category of sexual immorality.

The Torah considers adultery, promiscuity, prostitution, and sexual relationships outside of marriage as forms of sexual immorality. Sex out of wedlock, prostitution, and promiscuity all fall under the single Hebrew word *zanah*, ordinarily translated into English as "harlotry" or "whoredom." The actual meaning is far broader than acts of sex-for-hire. It includes any and all extra-marital sexual contact.[159]

Bibliography

Abegg, Martin, Edward Cook, and Michael Wise, ed. *The Dead Sea Scrolls: A New Translation*. San Francisco, CA: HarperSanFrancisco, 1996.

Aune, David. *The Westminster Dictionary of New Testament Early Christian Literature and Rhetoric*. Vol. 356. London, England: Westminster John Knox Press, 2003.

Bagatti, Bellarmino. *The Church from the Circumcision*. Jerusalem, Israel: Franciscan Printing Press, 1984.

Bar-Ron, Michael Shelomo. *Guide for the Noahide: A Complete Manual for Living by the Noahide Laws*. Springdale, AR: Lightcatcher Books, 2010.

Berkowitz, Ariel and D'vorah. *Torah Rediscovered*. Littleton, CO: First Fruits of Zion, 1996.

Bauckham , Richard. "James and the Jerusalem Church," in *The Book of Acts in Its Palestinian Setting*. Grand Rapids, MI: Wm. B. Eerdmans Publishing.

Bockmuehl, Markus. *Jewish Law in Gentile Churches: Halakhah and the Beginning of Christian Public Ethics*. Grand Rapids, MI: Baker Academic, 2000.

Bonhoeffer, Deitrich, *The Cost of Discipleship*. New York, NY: Collier Books, MacMillan Publishing, 1959.

Boyarin, Daniel. *Border Lines: The Partition of Judaeo-Christianity*. Philadelphia, PA: University of Pennsylvania Press, 2004.

Chrysostom, John: *Eight Homilies Against the Jews* (*Adversus Judaeos*). [Online at www.fordham.edu/halsall/source/chrysostom-jews6]

Clorfene, Chaim and Rogalsky, Yaakov. *The Path of the Righteous Gentile: An Introduction to the Seven Laws of the Children of Noah*. New York, NY: Feldheim Publishers, 1987.

Cohen, Abraham. *Everyman's Talmud*. New York, NY: Schocken Books, 1975.

Eby, Aaron., *Biblically Kosher: A Messianic Jewish Perspective on Kashrut*. Marshfield, MO: First Fruits of Zion, 2012.

Eby, Aaron. *First Steps in Messianic Jewish Prayer*. Marshfield, MO: First Fruits of Zion, 2014.

Eby, Aaron. "Rashbatz and the New Testament," *Messiah Journal* 103 (2010): 58–62.

Edersheim, Alfred. *The Life and Times of Jesus the Messiah*. Peabody, MA: Hendrickson Publishers,1995.

Epstein, Isidore. *Soncino Babylonian Talmud*. Brooklyn, NY: Judaica Press, 1990. CD-ROM edition. *Judaic Classics*. Chicago, IL: Davka Corporation, 1995.

Eusebius. *The History of the Church*. Translated by G.A. Williamson; Edited by Andrew Louth; Minneapolis, MN: Augsburg Publishing, 1965.

Fitzmeyer, Joseph. *The Acts of the Apostles: A New Translation with Introduction and Commentary*. The Anchor Bible; Garden City, NY: Doubleday, 1997.

Janicki, Toby. "The Ger Toshav: Residing within Israel," *Messiah Magazine* 120 (2015): 15–22.

Janicki, Toby. *Mezuzah*. Marshfield, MO: First Fruits of Zion, 2007.

Janicki, Toby. *Tefillin*. Marshfield, MO: First Fruits of Zion, 2010.

Janicki, Toby. *Tzitzit*. Marshfield, MO: First Fruits of Zion, 2009.

Heschel, Abraham Joshua. *The Sabbath*. New York, NY: Farrar, Straus and Giroux, 2005.

Heemstra, Marius. *The* Fiscus Judaicus *and the Parting of the Ways*. Tübingen, Germany: Mohr Siebeck, 2010.

Kaplan, Aryeh. *The Aryeh Kaplan Anthology Vol 2 (Waters of Eden)*. Brooklyn, NY. Mesorah Publications, Ltd. 1995.

Lachs, Samuel. *A Rabbinic Commentary on the New Testament: The Gospels of Matthew, Mark, and Luke*. Hoboken, NJ: Ktav Publishing House, 1987. . . .

Lancaster, D. Thomas. "The Birth of Yeshua at Sukkot: Evidence from an Old Source," *Messiah Journal* 111 (2012): 21–24.

Lancaster, D. Thomas. *The Sabbath Breaker: Jesus of Nazareth and Gospels' Sabbath Conflicts*. Marshfield, MO: First Fruits of Zion, 2013.

Lancaster, D. Thomas. *From Sabbath to Sabbath*. Marshfield, MO: First Fruits of Zion, forthcoming.

Lancaster, D. Thomas. *Torah Club: Chronicles of the Apostles*. 6 vols. Marshfield, MO: First Fruits of Zion, 2016.

Lancaster, D. Thomas. *Torah Club: Chronicles of the Messiah*. 6 vols. Marshfield, MO: First Fruits of Zion, 2014.

Lancaster, D. Thomas. *Holy Epistle to the Galatians*. Marshfield, MO: First Fruits of Zion, 2012.

Lancaster, D. Thomas. *Torah Club: Unrolling the Scroll*. 6 vols. Marshfield, MO: First Fruits of Zion, 2014.

Lancaster, D. Thomas. *What about the Sacrifices*. Marshfield, MO: First Fruits of Zion, 2010.

Lewis, C. S. *The Abolition of Man*. New York, NY: Harper Collins, 1974.

Lewis, C. S. *Mere Christianity*. New York, NY: Harper Collins, New York, 1980.

Lichtenstein, Yechiel Tzvi. *Beiur LeSiphrei Brit HaChadashah*. 8 vols. Translated by Professor G. Dahlman. Leipzig, Germany: 1897.

Lightfoot, J. B. and J. R. Harmer. *The Apostolic Fathers*. 2nd ed.; Edited by Michael Holmes; Grand Rapids, MI: Baker Books, 1989.

Roberts, Alexander and James Donaldson, eds. *The Ante-Nicene Fathers*. 10 vols. Peabody, MA: Hendrickson, 2004.

Robinson, Thomas. *Ignatius of Antioch and the Parting of the Ways: Early Jewish-Christian Relations*. Peabody, MA: Hendrickson Publishing, 2009.

Skarsaune, Oskar. *In the Shadow of the Temple*. Downers Grove, IL: InterVarsity Press, 2002.

Tomson, Peter. *Paul and the Jewish Law: Halakha in the Letters of the Apostle to the Gentiles* (Minneapolis, MN: Fortress Press, 1990), 180–181.

Weissman, Moshe. *The Midrash Says*. 5 vols. Brooklyn, NY: Bnay Yaakov Publications, 1980.

Weiner, Peter F. *Martin Luther, Hitler's Spiritual Ancestor*. Hutchinson & Co. Ltd. Online: www.tentmaker.org/books/MartinLuther-HitlersSpiritualAncestor.html#jews

Zetterholm, Magnus. *Approaches to Paul: A Student's Guide to Recent Scholarship*. Minneapolis, MN: Fortress Press, 2009.

Zetterholm, Magnus. *The Formation of Christianity in Antioch: A Social-Scientific Approach to the Separation Between Judaism and Christianity. London*, England: Routledge Tayor & Francis Group, 2005.

Endnotes

1 The Torah recognizes a legal category of non-Israelite that it refers to as the sojourner among the people. Certain laws and protections apply to the sojourner that do not apply to other Gentiles. See Toby Janicki, "The Ger Toshav: Residing within Israel," *Messiah Magazine* 120 (2015), 15–22.

2 For a study on the development of early Christianity and the church's separation from the synagogue during the first and second centuries, see D. Thomas Lancaster, "Birkat HaMinim" in *Torah Club: Chronicles of the Apostles* (Marshfield, MO: First Fruits of Zion, 2011).

3 b.*Brachot* 28b–29a.

4 Ignatius, *Epistle to the Magnesians* 9:2–3, long recension.

5 Justin Martyr, *Dialogue with Trypho,* 47.

6 Tertullian, *Against Marcion,* 4.5.

7 Eusebius, *Life of Constantine,* 3.18–19.

8 John Chrysostom, *Against the Jews,* Homily 1.5.

9 Romans 3:23

10 1 Corinthians 14:21.

11 John 10:34, 15:25.

12 Ephesians 2:12.

13 Genesis 9.

14 Exodus 29:9; Numbers 25:11–13.

15 Exodus 24:7.

16 For example, *Exodus Rabbah* 46:1.

17 b.*Shabbat* 31a.

18 1 John 3:4.

19 b.*Avodah Zarah* 8b.

20 m.*Makkot* 1:10.

21 Deuteronomy 17:6.

22 Abraham Cohen, *Everyman's Talmud*, (New York, NY: Schocken Books, 1975), 307.

23 *Susanna* (i.e., Daniel 14).

24 m.*Megillah* 4.2.

25 John 5:39.

26 Matthew 4:4.

27 Matthew 27:46.

28 Luke 24:44–45.

29 Acts 25:8, 28:17.

30 Hebrews 4:15.

31 Acts 7:38.

32 Hebrews 10:7.

33 2 Corinthians 3:12–18.

34 2 Timothy 3:16–17.

35 Luke 24:44.

36 Galatians 3:15–17.

37 Deuteronomy 13.

38 E.g., Ezekiel 14:6, 18:30.

39 E.g., Isaiah 2:3; Jeremiah 31:33–34.

40 E.g., Proverbs 28:4, 28:9, 29:18.

41 E.g., Psalm 119.

42 E.g., Matthew 4:17.

43 E.g., Matthew 5:17; Mark 7:9.

44 E.g., Matthew 5, 12:5, 22:32.

45 Matthew 5:17–19.

46 Revelation 12:17, 14:12.

47 Deuteronomy 13.

48 2 Timothy 3:16.

49 Exodus 20:2.

50 Lewis poses arguments for a universal sense of morality in works like *The Abolition of Man* and *Mere Christianity*.

51 Ezekiel 36:27–28.

52 Galatians 5:22–23.

53 Matthew 7:24–27.

54 Clement of Alexandria, *Stromata* 1.29.182.

55 b.*Sanhedrin* 68–70.

56 For an exposition on the seven laws and the broad scope that they encompass, see Chaim Clorfene and Yaakov Rogalsky, *The Path of the Righteous Gentile: An Introduction to the Seven Laws of the Children of Noah* (New York, NY: Feldheim Publishers, 1987); Michael Shelomo Bar-Ron, *Guide for the Noahide: A Complete Manual for Living by the Noahide Laws* (Springdale, AR: Lightcatcher Books, 2010).

57 Authorities disagree as to whether it is permissible for a Gentile to kill a fetus in order to save the life of a mother, but all agree that taking the mother's life to save the fetus is murder and punishable by the courts. Clorfene and Rogalsky, *The Path of the Righteous Gentile: An Introduction to the Seven Laws of the Children of Noah*, 81.

58 Cf. Matthew 5:22.

59 b.*Sanhedrin* 58.

60 t.*Avodah Zarah* 8:4.

61 E.g., Leviticus 3:17, 7:26, 7:10–16, 19:26.

62 David Rudolph, "Paul's 'Rule in All the Churches'" (1 Cor 7:17–24) and Torah-Defined Ecclesiological Variegation." *Studies in Christian-Jewish Relations* 5 (2010): 1–23.

63 Acts 15:7, Western Text.

64 E.g., m.*Avot* 3:5.

65 b.*Yoma* 85b.

66 b.*Yevamot* 47b.

67 b.*Sanhedrin* 94b. One who returns to Torah takes upon himself "the yoke of repentance" (b.*Moed Katan* 16b).

68 Richard Bauckham, "James and the Jerusalem Church," in *The Book of Acts in Its Palestinian Setting* (Richard Bauckham, ed.; Grand Rapids, MI: Wm. B. Eerdmans Publishing Co., 1995), 459.

69 That which is torn (*terefah*) and that which died of its own (*nevelah*), i.e., carcasses (e.g., Leviticus 22:8).

70 Deuteronomy 14:21; Leviticus 17:12–13.

71 t.*Avodah Zarah* 8:4.

72 Luke 10:29–37.

73 E.g., Romans 12:10, 12:16, 13:8, 14:13, 15:71; 1 Corinthians 11:33; Galatians 5:13, 5:26; Ephesians 4:1–2, 4:32; Colossians 3:9; 1 Thessalonians 5:15; Hebrews 3:13, 10:24–25; James 4:11, 5:9; 1 Peter 1:22, 4:9–10; 2 John 1:5–6.

74 Luke 4:16.

75 Matthew 5:17–20; John 14:15–21.

76 Yechiel Tzvi Lichtenstein, *Commentary on the New Testament: The Acts of the Apostles* (Unpublished, Marshfield, MO: Vine of David,

2010), on Acts 15; originally published in Hebrew: *Beiur LeSiphrei Brit HaChadashah* (Leipzig, Germany: Professor G. Dahlman, 1897).

77 Rabbi Jacob Emden's Letter, *Seder Olam Rabba Vezutta*. Rabbi Jacob Emden (Yavetz, 1697–1776), a leading Torah authority and scholar, wrote a letter to a Jewish council in Poland that spoke of Yeshua and Christianity in a remarkably positive light. This letter was later published in a work called *Seder Olam Rabba Vezutta*.

78 Translation of *Keshet Umagen* from Aaron Eby, "Rashbatz and the New Testament," *Messiah Journal* 103 (2010): 58–62.

79 Leviticus 17; Deuteronomy 12.

80 Colossians 2:16–17.

81 Deuteronomy 5:15.

82 Exodus 20:11.

83 Colossians 2:16–17.

84 For example, b.*Sanhedrin* 97a.

85 Deuteronomy 5:15.

86 For discussion about Yeshua's conflicts regarding healing on the Sabbath, see D. Thomas Lancaster, *The Sabbath Breaker: Jesus of Nazareth and Gospels' Sabbath Conflicts* (Marshfield, MO: First Fruits of Zion, 2013) and discussions in *Torah Club: Chronicles of the Messiah* on pertinent passages. See also D. Thomas Lancaster, *From Sabbath to Sabbath* (Marshfield, MO: First Fruits of Zion, forthcoming).

87 Revelation 1:10.

88 Luke 4:16.

89 Leviticus 23:3.

90 Luke 15:1.

91 John 5:17.

92 Matthew 24:20.

93 Acts 15:21.

94 Leviticus 23:10–11

95 m.*Menachot* 10:3. See m.*Menachot* 10 for detailed information on the omer ritual.

96 b.*Shabbat* 88b; e.g., *Exodus Rabbah* 5:9; Moshe Weissman, *The Midrash Says: The Book of Shemos*, vol. 2 (Brooklyn, NY: Bnay Yaakov Publications, 1995), 182 citing *Midrash Chazit*. See D. Thomas Lancaster, *Torah Club: Chronicles of the Apostles* (Marshfield, MO: First Fruits of Zion, 2011) on Acts 2.

97 Acts 20:16.

98 Leviticus 23:42–43.

99 Micah 4:4; Zechariah 3:10.

100 Isaiah 4:5–6.

101 According to *Aggadta DeShim'on Kefa*, early Jewish believers associated the Messiah's birth with the first day of Sukkot and His circumcision with the eighth day. See D. Thomas Lancaster, "The Birth of Yeshua at Sukkot: Evidence from an Old Source," *Messiah Journal* 111 (2012): 21–24; *Torah Club: Chronicles of the Messiah* (Marshfield, MO: First Fruits of Zion, 2014), A17–A22.

102 *Didache* 8:3.

103 See Aaron Eby, *First Steps in Messianic Jewish Prayer* (Marshfield, MO: First Fruits of Zion, 2014).

104 See the laws of Leviticus 15 and 18.

105 Leviticus 15:5-14, 31.

106 Romans 6:3–5.

107 Matthew 9:20; Mark 6:56. See Toby Janicki, *Tzitzit* (Marshfield, MO: First Fruits of Zion, 2009).

108 See Toby Janicki, *Mezuzah* (Marshfield, MO: First Fruits of Zion, 2007).

109 Deuteronomy 6:9.

110 See Toby Janicki, *Tefillin* (Marshfield, MO: First Fruits of Zion, 2010).

111 For further study about the Bible's dietary laws, see Aaron Eby, *Biblically Kosher: A Messianic Jewish Perspective on Kashrut* (Marshfield, MO: First Fruits of Zion, 2012).

112 Genesis 8:15–9:13.

113 See the appendix, "The Apostolic Decree," for more information on the Bible's dietary standards for Gentile disciples.

114 Deuteronomy 6:4–9.

115 *Exodus Rabbah* 6:1.

116 Deitrich Bonhoeffer , *The Cost of Discipleship*, (New York, NY: Collier Books, MacMillan Publishing, 1959).

117 Idolatry—Deuteronomy 7:25, 13:14, 17:1–4, 20:18. Child sacrifice—Deuteronomy 12:31. Divination, sorcery, witchcraft, spell casting, channeling spirits and consulting the dead—Deuteronomy 8:10–12. Sexual immorality in worship—Deuteronomy 23:18. Cross-dressing—Deuteronomy 22:5. Re-remarriage—Deuteronomy 24:4. False weights and measures—Deuteronomy 25:15–16.

118 Deuteronomy 12:13–14.

119 Acts 2:46, 3:1, 5:42, 21:26, 25:8.

120 See Aaron Eby, *Biblically Kosher: A Messianic Jewish Perspective on Kashrut* (Marshfield, MO: First Fruits of Zion , 2012).

121 Deuteronomy 12:13–14. See D. Thomas Lancaster, *What about the Sacrifices?* (Marshfield, MO: First Fruits of Zion, 2010).

122 Exodus 18:13ff; Deuteronomy 17:6–13.

123 Matthew 23:2–3.

124 The Greek *paradosis* (tradition) refers to an oral tradition handed down through the generations. The New Testament often uses the word to describe rabbinic tradition and interpretation—the pre-Mishnaic body of oral law: Matthew 15:6, 23; Mark 7:3, 5, 8–9, 13; Galatians 1:14. It can also refer to apostolic teaching transmitted orally: 1 Corinthians 11:2; 2 Thessalonians 2:15, 3:6.

125 m.*Pirkei Avot* 1:1.

126 Deuteronomy 8:10.

127 For a more thorough study of the hand-washing incident, see D. Thomas Lancaster, *Torah Club: Chronicles of the Messiah*, vol. 3 (Marshfield, MO: First Fruits of Zion, 2014), 741–772.

128 Numbers 19.

129 Cf. m.*Yadayim* 2:4.

130 Rabbi Abbahu's opinion in b.*Sotah* 5a citing Ezekiel 4:13.

131 Exodus 35:3.

132 1 Corinthians 7:17–18.

133 Acts 18:18.

134 The term "the commandment" is a synonym for Torah.

135 The term "good work" or "good deed" refers to observing the commandments of the Torah.

136 See D. Thomas Lancaster, *Holy Epistle to the Galatians* (Marshfield, MO: First Fruits of Zion, 2012).

137 b.*Sanhedrin* 43a.

138 This story is told in *Oznayim LaTorah* and cited in Moshe Weissman, *The Midrash Says: The Book of Devarim* (vol. 5; Brooklyn, NY: Bnay Yaakov Publications, 1985), 172.

139 E.g., 1 Corinthians 10:14, 12:2 and 1 Thessalonians 1:9–10; see tractate *Avodah Zarah* in *Tosefta*, Mishnah, and Talmud.

140 Exodus 34:15.

141 Revelation 2:14, 20.

142 Peter Tomson, *Paul and the Jewish Law: Halakha in the Letters of the Apostle to the Gentiles* (Minneapolis, MN: Fortress Press, 1990), 180–181.

143 Justin Martyr, *Dialogue with Trypho* 35.

144 *Didache* 6:3.

145 Minucius Felix, *Octavius* 30.

146 Tertullian, *Apology* 9:13.

147 "'Things strangled' (πνικτων) are prohibited in Leviticus 17:13. The difficulty with this term in the apostolic decree has arisen simply because Leviticus 17:13 is a positive prescription: that animals killed for eating must be slaughtered in such a way that their blood drains out. Abstention from πνικτων is the negative corollary, for an animal killed in such a way that the blood remains 'chocked.'" See Bauckham, "James and the Jerusalem Church," 459.

148 m.*Chullin* 1:2.

149 Philo, *The Special Law* 4:122; *Joseph and Asenath* 8:5.

150 John B. Polhill, *Acts* (The New American Commentary 26; David S. Dockery et. al., eds.; Nashville, TN: Broadman & Holman Publishers, 2001), 330.

151 Fitzmyer, *The Acts of the Apostles: A New Translation with Introduction and Commentary*, 557.

152 Tomson, *Paul and the Jewish Law*, 178–179.

153 *Shechitah* (שחיטה) involves the precise slitting of the jugular veins (but not the esophagus) and other regulations. The sages insist that the method of slaughter originated at Mount Sinai. They find an allusion to this in Deuteronomy 12:2: "You may slaughter ... as I have commanded you." To the sages this meant that God showed Moses and the children of Israel the correct way to slaughter the meat.

154 Tertullian, *Apology* 9:13.

155 Oskar Skarsaune (*In the Shadow of the Temple* [Downers Grove, IL: InterVarsity Press, 2002], 239) cites the story in *Ecclesiastical History* (5.1.26) about the martyrs of Lyons who were accused of cannibalism and blood libel:

> Under torture, a girl named Biblias in a sudden burst of indignation said, "How can those eat children, who are forbidden to eat the blood even of brute beasts?" This clearly indicates that the community of Lyons [France] still observed the apostolic decree of Acts 15 concerning kosher meat ... The question arises, where did the Christians get their meat from? The only possible answer is from a kosher market established for the Jews and Christians in the City.

156 Yechiel Tzvi Lichtenstein, *Commentary on the New Testament: The Acts of the Apostles* (Unpublished, Marshfield, MO: Vine of David, 2010), on Acts 15:20; originally published in Hebrew: *Beiur LeSiphrei Brit HaChadashah* (Leipzig, Germany: Professor G. Dahlman, 1897).

157 1 Thessalonians 5:22. Cf. 1Timothy 2:9–10; 1 Corinthians 7:1–2.

158 Deuteronomy 22:5.

159 E.g., Genesis 34:31, 38:24; Leviticus 19:29, 21:7, 9, 14; Numbers 25:1; Deuteronomy 22:21.